T0114841

GET A GRIP
—— ON THE ——
BIBLE

A Study Guide:
Genesis through Ruth

GET A GRIP-ON THE BIBLE – ONE OF THREE

JERRY L. BURTON

WESTBOW
PRESS®
A DIVISION OF THOMAS NELSON
& ZONDERVAN

Copyright © 2020 Jerry L. Burton.

All rights reserved. No part of this book may be used or reproduced by any means, graphic, electronic, or mechanical, including photocopying, recording, taping or by any information storage retrieval system without the written permission of the author except in the case of brief quotations embodied in critical articles and reviews.

This book is a work of non-fiction. Unless otherwise noted, the author and the publisher make no explicit guarantees as to the accuracy of the information contained in this book and in some cases, names of people and places have been altered to protect their privacy.

WestBow Press books may be ordered through booksellers or by contacting:

WestBow Press
A Division of Thomas Nelson & Zondervan
1663 Liberty Drive
Bloomington, IN 47403
www.westbowpress.com
844-714-3454

Because of the dynamic nature of the Internet, any web addresses or links contained in this book may have changed since publication and may no longer be valid. The views expressed in this work are solely those of the author and do not necessarily reflect the views of the publisher, and the publisher hereby disclaims any responsibility for them.

Any people depicted in stock imagery provided by Getty Images are models, and such images are being used for illustrative purposes only. Certain stock imagery © Getty Images.

Scripture quotations are taken from The Holy Bible, New International Version®, NIV® Copyright © 1973, 1978, 1984, 2011 by Biblica, Inc.® Used by permission. All rights reserved worldwide.

Library of Congress Control Number: 2020917778

ISBN: 978-1-6642-0552-9 (sc)
ISBN: 978-1-6642-0551-2 (hc)
ISBN: 978-1-6642-0553-6 (e)

Library of Congress Control Number: 2020917778

Print information available on the last page.

WestBow Press rev. date: 11/03/2020

CONTENTS

DEDICATION

To Kiana Rebecca Caalim, one of my former students at Hope Christian School in Albuquerque, NM. Her healing is complete as she rests in the arms of her Savior!

ACKNOWLEDGEMENTS

To my good friend, Anthony Valdez, who has helped me edit my manuscript and to all the men in my Small Group who have encouraged and inspired me in this endeavor.

To my lovely gift from God, my wife, Laura, for all the long discussions, the endless patience, and the love for me that she shows every minute of every day. I thank God for her and for all of her godly traits and wisdom.

INTRODUCTION

Have you ever picked up the Bible and looked at it without opening it? Have you thought, *Wow, this is a huge book!*

Then you open it. *Wow, that's really small print!*

You ask yourself, "Do I really think I can understand this? Do I really have time to read all this?"

Then you put the Bible down, thinking, *Some other time!*

I have written this study guide just for you.

My mom was a storyteller. When I was only five years old, she had her own radio program. The elementary schools in town would send children into her studio each day. Mom would read fairy tales and Bible stories to them while she was on the air.

Mom practiced her storytelling on me. I look back on those days and realize that my retention was great when I heard or read a story. Most people respond well to stories.

In the study guide for each book, Genesis through Ruth, I give you information in story form.

1. I start with a small amount of background information about the book: its author, when it was written, who the intended audience was, a little about the time it was written, and what

was going on in the world culturally and historically during that time.

2. I tell you one or two short stories from the book and explain a few things along the way. I start with stories you may have heard before. Then I tell one or two stories you may not have heard before. I try to keep it simple. There's always a point to be made in scripture. I try to identify the point for you.

3. Sometimes, after I have given you some background information, I ask you to read a story on your own. This will help you build your confidence in your ability to read scripture.

4. I give you some discussion questions in the event that you are reading this book in a study group.

5. I give you a list of topics covered in the book so you have an overview of its contents.

My goal for you is to remember just one or two main ideas from each book of the Bible from Genesis through Ruth.

May God bless you through the reading of His marvelous Word!

CHAPTER 1
GENESIS

In this chapter, you will get a grip on who God is, who we are relative to Him, and how much He loves us and wants love from us.

Genesis, the first book in the Bible, is one of five books of the Bible referred to as the Pentateuch: Genesis, Exodus, Leviticus, Numbers, and Deuteronomy. In these books, the key idea to remember is that God is revealing Himself to His people. He is also revealing the rules (laws) of the relationship between Him and them.

SECTION 1—REVIEW

In subsequent chapters, this section will contain a short review, or summary, of the previous chapters. This will help you see the connection of each book to the next.

SECTION 2—PREFACE

In Genesis, you will read about the creation of all things and the spiritual being, God, who created all things. You will also read about two covenants. A covenant is an agreement similar to a legal contract. One of the covenants was between God and Noah. The other covenant was between God and Abram.

The story line in Genesis moves from a purely spiritual realm, before creation, into what we perceive as a physical realm, after creation. There is at least one universe (a human term with human limitations), with galaxies, stars, solar systems, planets, and more. All were created by God. Both the spiritual and the physical realms coexist and overlap.

It is generally accepted, based on Moses's account, that humankind's journey began in the eastern region of Mesopotamia, or present-day Iraq. Looking at Figure 1.1, humans started life's journey perhaps at location 1.

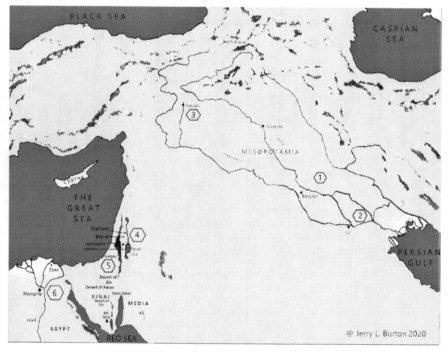

Figure 1.1. Mesopotamia

After some unspecified period of time, the man, Adam, was taken by God and put into a garden, which God Himself had "planted." Now we are at location 2 on the map. Again, we aren't told how long Adam and his new "bride," Eve, were in the garden communing in a wonderfully personal way with God.

Enter Satan, the adversary and tempter. Now the road gets rough. After banishment from the garden, humans make many mistakes, which result in some interesting stories. In all these stories, God reveals more and more about who He is, who we were meant to be, and how God and humankind are meant to relate to each other.

Over a long period of time, humankind spreads out beyond Mesopotamia. Humans' relationship with God becomes more diluted. But one man, Abram, is noticed by God. Abram's story ranges from Ur, where he was born, to Harran, location 3, where his family moved. It is here that God calls Abram to become the patriarch of the Israelite nation.

From Harran, the stories move southward through Shechem and Bethel, location 4, then toward the Negev, location 5. Due to a famine in the land, Abram eventually goes all the way to Egypt, location 6.

The map will lead you through the remainder of the book of Genesis, eventually ending with a man named Joseph in Egypt.

There are numerous stories along the way—some sad, some funny, and some very scary. You will read four short stories about four major events: "In the Beginning," "The Fall of Man," "The Flood," and "The Scattering of the Nations." These stories are from the pre-patriarchal period and take place in Mesopotamia.

The second part of Genesis tells us about many people, but our focus will be on four. You will read the stories of these four patriarchs (fathers) of the nation of Israel: Abraham (Abram), Isaac, Jacob, and Joseph. As you read these stories, ask yourself two questions:

1. What is God willing to do for humankind?
2. What is God asking humankind to do for Him?

SECTION 3—GENERAL

Author:[1] Moses, by historical tradition, is assumed to be the man who wrote the book of Genesis. He lived from 1526 BC to 1406 BC (120 years).[2]

Date Written:[3] Probably between 1440 and 1400 BC. Moses was about eighty years[4] old at the time he led a group of slaves out of Egypt at the command of God. All these slaves were descendants of Abraham, Isaac (one of Abraham's sons), and Jacob (one of Isaac's sons). Moses and the ex-slaves were in the desert (between 1440 BC and 1400 BC) when Moses started writing Genesis.

All the events in Genesis had occurred before Moses was born. The information Moses wrote in Genesis most likely came from two sources:[5]

1. direct revelation from God and
2. information that had been passed down to the slaves, including his own mother, and told to Moses.

Period Covered:[6] Before creation to around 1805 BC (death of Joseph).

Audience:[7] God told Moses to write the book of Genesis so these people from Egypt would know who God was and understand their national and spiritual heritage.

Cultural Setting:[8] Genesis covers an unknown length of time and cultural development. By the time of the writing of Genesis, civilizations were very well developed. There were large cities and nations ruled by pharaohs and kings. The eastern Mediterranean area, North Africa, and Near East (Eastern Europe and Western Asia) were engaged in trade and kept very sophisticated records of contracts and daily transactions, and they communicated extensively with each other much as we do today, but without the technology.

Historical Setting:[9] The historical setting of Genesis is impossible to state, at least for the first eleven chapters. History before the age of writing is, of course, unrecorded. The earliest records we have of any civilization are that of the Sumerians. They dominated Mesopotamia from roughly 2900 to 2350 BC. During this time, civilization was developing. Urbanization, or the creation of centers of living like towns and cities, took place. Also, there they developed the foundations of mathematics, astronomy, law, and medicine. All this was before the birth of Abraham! Abraham is thought to have been born in 2166 BC.[10]

The center of power shifted throughout the region numerous times. Just before 2100 BC, the city of Ur took prominence in southern Mesopotamia.

After that, during the period ranging from about 2000–1600 BC, the Babylonians gained power over the other city-states. Most of the stories in Genesis 12–50 take place during this time.

SECTION 4—FOUR GREAT EVENTS

A. The Creation of the Universe; Adam and Eve
Genesis 1–2

The creation story accounts for the creation of the universe as we know it. The first verse in the Bible says, "In the beginning, God." I think this is the most important part of the creation story.

God existed prior to creating the physical heavens and earth. He existed then and still does exist with other "heavenly hosts." Sometimes we refer to these as angels. God was not created, but He did create everything else, and He said His creation was good.

We don't know how long it took God to create everything. God has no time—He just is and can create things as if they are brand-new or as if they are very old by humankind's limited standard.

With the LORD a day is like a thousand years, and a thousand years are like a day. (2 Peter 3:8 NIV)[11]

God created Adam and Eve (and all humankind) after He created the earth and everything else in it. Humankind was created in God's image and was given the responsibility for caring for all the other forms of life, the animals and plants created by God.

No one knows for sure where God created humans. A lot of people think it happened in Mesopotamia. Look at location 1. The ruins and artifacts found by archaeologists in this area are the oldest found anywhere on earth, so this area probably is close to where God created humankind.

At the end of the second chapter of Genesis, it appears that God had made man, planted a garden somewhere east of the creation spot, and then put man in the garden. This is referred to as the garden of Eden. It was there that God created woman. Look at location 2.

In Genesis 3:8, we are told that God walked in the garden in the cool of the day. He physically fellowshipped with His creation. God called out to Adam and Eve. He also communicated aloud with them, and they had conversation similar to Moses and God in the tent of meeting. You will learn about that in Exodus.

Take a moment and try to visualize God, Adam, Eve, and yourself in the midst of God's creation, having a nice talk. It is this relationship that God called "very good." Please remember this mental picture and carry it with you as you proceed through this study. This is the way God intended our relationship with Him to be.

B. The Fall and the Results of Sin
Genesis 3–5

God had heavenly beings around Him, but they were like servants to Him. Humankind, on the other hand, was created to be good friends with God and was given free will. This meant that humankind did not have to be servants to God. They could choose to love God or not love God. They could choose to obey Him or not to obey Him.

God wanted humankind to obey Him out of love. It's important to understand, though, one way that God measured our love for Him was by how much we chose to obey Him.

Humans were created like God, but not as gods. Adam was told by God that he could eat the fruit of any tree in the garden of Eden, except the one that was called the tree of the knowledge of good and evil. God told Adam that he would die if he ate the fruit of that tree.

One day, Satan, in the form of a serpent, tempted Eve to eat the fruit of the forbidden tree so she could be like God. Satan said,

> For God knows that when you eat from it your eyes will be opened, and you will be like God, knowing good and evil. (Genesis 3:5 NIV)[12]

Adam and Eve ate the fruit because they chose not to believe God, and because they wanted to be like God, knowing the difference between good and evil. But of course, Satan had lied—they did not become gods. By disobeying God, they had committed sin. They became sinners, they became ashamed, and the penalty for disobedience was to grow old and die.

The penalty for sin is death. God removed Adam and Eve from the garden to keep them from eating fruit from the tree of life, which would cause them to live forever in a sinful condition. If that happened, they would never again be able to fellowship with God. Satan knew sin would separate humans from God. That was what Satan wanted.

We don't know for sure where Adam and Eve went after that, but it probably was not far from the garden.

C. The Flood
Genesis 6:9–10:32

Humankind continued to sin. They eventually rejected God and started believing in gods or strange things that they didn't understand. Some of these strange gods were planets and stars. Some of them were other natural things like wind, fire, ice, and the sky. Humans worshipped God's creation but not God, the Creator. Eventually, God became sorry that He had created humans.

However, there was one man who was righteous and blameless when compared to all the other people. That man's name was Noah. God decided not to destroy Noah and his family, but the rest of the people were going to die.

We don't have any record of where Noah and his family were living at the time of the flood. More than likely, I believe they were somewhere in the vicinity of the Euphrates and Tigris Rivers. That is the area that would support many, if not all, life forms of the age. Also, that is the area that would hide the "springs of the deep" mentioned in verse 8:2.

God told Noah to build an ark, a large boat. He told Noah exactly how big the boat should be and that it had to have room for animals of all kinds. When the ark was finished, God sent the animals to Noah, and they were loaded into the ark. Then Noah, his wife, and his three sons and their wives got in the ark. According to verse 7:16, God Himself shut the door after them.

Then God sent the rain, and the springs began to gush forth. It rained for forty days, and all the earth was flooded.

After it quit raining, it was 150 days before the floodwaters went down. Finally, dry land appeared. Almost two months later, the earth was completely dry, and God told Noah to come out of the ark and let all the animals go. Look again at the map. Close to the middle of the top border of the map, between the headwaters of the Tigris and Euphrates Rivers, is Mount Ararat (verse 8:4).

Noah built an altar and sacrificed burnt offerings on it to the Lord. God was pleased and made the following covenant with Noah concerning future destruction of humans. The sign God gave us was the rainbow.

> The LORD smelled the pleasing aroma and said in his heart: "Never again will I curse the ground because of humans, even though every inclination of the human heart is evil from childhood. And never again will I destroy all living creatures, as I have done." (Genesis 8:21 NIV)[13]

Noah's three sons Shem, Ham, and Japheth, and their families repopulated the world. Genesis 10 details their migration patterns. To summarize their movements, Shem's descendants repopulated the area we know as the Middle East. Ham's descendants repopulated Egypt and most of Africa. Japheth's descendants repopulated what is generally known as Europe.

There's much more to it than that, but there is one son of Shem who is very important to the history of Israel. That son is Canaan. In Genesis 9:20–27, Ham, the youngest son of Noah, was very disrespectful to Noah. Noah cursed Ham's youngest son, Canaan, in response. Many of Canaan's descendants eventually settled in the land called Canaan. This is the same land that God later promised to the nation of Israel as the Promised Land.

D. The Scattering of the Nations
Genesis 11:1–9

After the world had become well populated again, people began moving eastward, where there was more room. All the people spoke the same language. They had become very good builders. They no longer used stones but instead used baked bricks, which were held together with tar.

They found a good place to settle and decided to build themselves a large city with a tower that reached to the "heavens."

Figure 1.2. Ziggurat

The kind of tower they were going to build was common in those times and was called a ziggurat. The structure was solid and had no interior space.

There were usually stairways or ramps that led to the top of the structure. At the top, there was a small room with a bed and a table set for the deity.[14]

The purpose of the tower was to provide a place for a deity to take up his residence among the people.[15] It did not serve as a place of worship. The reference to "up to the heavens" probably had more to do with the deity coming down to dwell among the people than the people going up and invading the heavenly realm of the gods.

The people had given the following reason for building the tower.

> So that we may make a name for ourselves; otherwise
> we will be scattered over the face of the earth. (Genesis
> 11:4 NIV)[16]

Many of the people of that time believed that the quality of the afterlife depended, to a large degree, on the deceased being remembered by the living members of the family. If those living family members, generation after generation, mentioned the name of the deceased, that was thought to add to the vitality of the afterlife. If the deceased was not remembered, it was as if he or she had been "scattered over the face of the earth" and had never existed.[17]

When I consider this story, I can't help but feel that we still have a human need to be remembered after we die. Perhaps some evidence for this is captured in the tombstones, the dedication plaques in buildings, and on statues and other structures. However, I doubt that the mentioning of my name after I die could add anything to the quality of my afterlife if I'm dwelling in the presence of Christ, my Savior!

> But the LORD came down to see the city and the tower the people were building. The LORD said, "If as one people speaking the same language they have begun to do this, then nothing they plan to do will be impossible for them. Come, let us go down and confuse their language so they will not understand each other."
> So the LORD scattered them from there over all the earth, and they stopped building the city. That is why it was called Babel—because there the LORD confused the language of the whole world. From there the LORD scattered them over the face of the whole earth. (Genesis 11:5–9 NIV)[18]

The people who spoke the same language probably chose to stay together as they moved from one area to another.

It is assumed that the tower of Babel was in or near Babylon. There are many such towers, or ziggurats, in Mesopotamia, so it is hard to claim any one of them as *the* tower of Babel.

Note the position of Babylon on the map, just to the left and down from location 1. in Figure 1.1.

SECTION 5—THE PATRIARCHS
(FATHERS OF THE FAITH)

A. Abraham
Genesis 11:27–20:18

The name given to Abraham at birth was Abram. Later, God changed his name to Abraham.

Abram was born in Ur around 2166 BC, during the Middle Bronze Age in the Mediterranean area. Ur was a very important city. Abram and his family were probably wealthy. Abram later moved to the city of Harran.

On the map, Ur is located to the lower left of location 2. Harran is located to the upper right of location 3.

When in Harran, God called Abram to serve Him. The Lord said to Abram,

> Leave your country, your people and your father's household and go to the land I will show you. I will make you a great nation and I will bless you. (Genesis 12:1–2 NIV)[19]

Abram, then seventy-five years old, left Harran with his wife, Sarai, and his nephew Lot. They took all their possessions, including their servants, and set out for the land of Canaan. Eventually, they arrived there. Canaan is the long, narrow area to the left of location 4.

B. God's Covenant with Abram
Genesis 15:1–23

Abram and his wife had waited about ten years and still had no children. God came to Abram in a vision and Abram asked God about the promise of children.

It was still dark outside, and God took Abram out and told him,

> Look up at the heavens and count the stars – if indeed
> you can count them. So shall your offspring be. (Genesis
> 15:5 NIV)[20]

The next verse says,

> Abram believed the LORD, and He credited it to him as
> righteousness. (Genesis 15:6 NIV)[21]

The Lord reassured Abram that the land (Canaan) God had promised him would be given to him.

Abram asked God how he could be sure that he would take possession of it.

Then God did something amazing. To help Abram trust Him, God set up a ceremony for God and Abram to perform together. The ceremony was a common one in that culture. It was performed whenever two persons "solemnized a covenant" between them.[22]

The Lord told Abram to bring Him a heifer, a goat, and a ram, each three years old, along with a dove and a young pigeon.

Abram cut the heifer, goat, and ram in half. The halves of each animal were placed across from each other. The dove and the pigeon were not cut in half.

Each party to the contract had to walk through the blood between the parts of the dead animals. As they went, they would say something like, "If I fail to keep my part of this contract, may I become as these animals." The stronger party to the contract always walked through first. Then the other party would walk through. Jeremiah 34:18 references such a ceremony.

As the sun was setting, Abram fell into a deep sleep. A thick darkness came over Abram. The Lord said to Abram,

> Know for certain that your descendants will be strangers in a country not their own, and they will be enslaved and mistreated for four hundred years. But I will punish the nation they serve as slaves, and afterward they will come out with great possessions. You, however, will go to your fathers in peace and be buried at a good old age. In the fourth generation your descendants will come back here, for the sin of the Amorites has not yet reached its full measure. (Genesis 15:13–16 NIV)[23]

The Amorites, according to Genesis 10:15–16, were descendants from Canaan.

When darkness had fallen, a smoking firepot and a blazing torch appeared and passed between the pieces of dead animals. The smoke represented God. After the smoking firepot had passed through, Abram should have passed through. But he didn't—he was in a deep sleep.

God knew that Abram and his people could not keep their part of the contract—to be a holy people set apart for the glory of God. If Abram had passed through, he and all his descendants would have to die, and there would be no nation of Israel.

The blazing torch, also God, passed through in Abram's place. By doing so, God had committed Himself to die in place of Abram and his people as payment for their sins.

And in the form of His only Son, Christ Jesus, God did die for the sins of all humankind! God Himself paid the debt!

This wonderful story demonstrates God's love for and faithfulness to us. In this story, you can graphically see the future coming of Jesus to pay for our sins.

But there is something else this story demonstrates about God. God used a ceremony that was common to the people of that time. He did that so Abram would fully understand the commitment God was making and that God was binding Himself to that commitment.

You will see, as you go through this workbook series, many other examples of God doing things in "human" ways. It is God's way of meeting us where we are so that we can fully understand.

C. Abram's Name Change
Genesis 17:1–16

When Abram was ninety-nine years old and Sarai was ninety years old, they still had not had children. God restated His promise to Abram. God said,

> You will be the father of many nations. (Genesis 17:4 NIV)[24]

God changed Abram's name to Abraham and Sarai's name to Sarah. Nine months later, Isaac, their son was born.

D. Abraham Tested
Genesis 22:1–19

When Isaac was a young boy, God told Abraham to take him up to a mountain and sacrifice him as a burnt offering. In ancient Near East cultures, it was uncommon, but not unheard of, for people to sacrifice their children to pagan gods.

Abraham and two of his servants cut some wood for the fire and placed it on a donkey. Then they set out with the donkey and Isaac toward the mountain. The mountain range was the Moriah Mountains. On the map, that would be somewhere between Jerusalem and the middle of location 5 and between the Dead Sea and the Great Sea.

When they came to the bottom of the mountain, Abraham told the servants to stay with the donkey. He placed the wood on Isaac, who then carried it up the mountain as Abraham carried the fire and a knife.

As they climbed up the mountain, Isaac said to his father,

> Father! The fire and wood are here, but where is the lamb for the burnt offering? (Genesis 22:7 NIV)[25]

Abraham answered,

> God himself will provide the lamb for the burnt offering, my son. (Genesis 22:8 NIV)[26]

When they reached the top, Abraham built an altar and laid the firewood on it. He bound his son and laid him on top of the wood. Then Abraham drew his knife to slay Isaac.

But an angel called out to Abraham from heaven and told him to stop.

> "Do not lay a hand on the boy," he said. "Do not do anything to him. Now I know that you fear God, because you have not withheld from me your son, your only son." (Genesis 22:12 NIV)[27]

Abraham looked up and saw a ram whose horns were caught in the thicket. Abraham used the ram as his offering.

In this story, we again see the parts of God's plan that become fulfilled in Jesus Christ.

Abraham was the father with an only son, Isaac.

God was the Father of an only Son, Jesus.

Abraham was willing to give his only son as a sacrifice to receive forgiveness for his sins. He believed that God would resurrect Isaac or replace him.

God was willing to give His only Son as a sacrifice for the forgiveness of our sins, and Jesus was resurrected.

E. Isaac
Genesis 24:1–67

When Isaac turned forty, he was old enough to marry. He married a woman named Rebekah.

When Isaac had reached sixty years old, Rebekah had not yet given birth to any children.

> Isaac prayed to the LORD on behalf of his wife, so that she might have children. The LORD answered his prayer, and his wife Rebekah became pregnant. (Genesis 25:21 NIV)[28]

Rebekah gave birth to twin boys, Esau and Jacob. Esau was born first and therefore, because he was the oldest, was the heir to the birthright. Birthright means you get a "double portion" of the property and things owned by your parents when they died.

F. Jacob
Genesis 27:1–37:1

One day, Esau returned from hunting. He had been gone for a long time and was very hungry. Jacob was making some of his delicious red stew. Jacob offered to sell the stew to Esau for his birthright. Esau was so hungry that he agreed.

Many years later, Isaac, very old and mostly blind, called Esau to his bedside. Then he told Esau to go hunt and bring back some wild game for him to eat. Isaac told Esau that when he returned, he would give Esau his blessing before he died. The blessing was the method of giving the inheritance to the oldest son. Esau got his bow and quiver and left to go hunt.

But Rebekah, who favored Jacob, had overheard what Isaac had said to Esau.

After Esau left to go hunt, Rebekah told Jacob to bring her some wild game. Then she made some goat stew and some bread, and she dressed Jacob in Esau's clothes. Esau was very hairy and Jacob was not, so she put goat skins on Jacob's arms and neck. That way, if Isaac touched Jacob's arm or neck, he would think it was Esau.

When Jacob approached Isaac and told his father that he was Esau, Isaac did not believe him. He asked Jacob to come near so he could touch him. When Isaac touched Jacob's arm, he said,

> The voice is the voice of Jacob, but the hands are the hands of Esau. (Genesis 27:22 NIV)[29]

Isaac was not convinced it was Esau who had come to him, so he asked that the wild game be brought to him so he could taste it. Jacob gave Isaac the stew and bread and some wine. Then Isaac said to him,

> Come here, my son, and kiss me. (Genesis 27:26 NIV)[30]

When Jacob kissed Isaac, Isaac smelled the clothes Jacob was wearing. They were Esau's clothes, so Isaac gave the blessing to Jacob instead of to Esau. Then Jacob quickly left.

Just after Jacob left, Esau returned. Both Isaac and Esau were extremely upset when they realized what Jacob had done.

Esau was very bitter and decided to wait until after Isaac died to kill Jacob. Rebekah heard of it and told Jacob to run away and live with her brother Laban. Laban lived in Harran, the town where Isaac's servant had found Rebekah.

After a month at Laban's house, Laban offered to pay Jacob for the work Jacob had been doing for him. Laban asked Jacob what would be a fair wage. Laban had two daughters. Leah, the older daughter, had "weak eyes," but Rachel was lovely in form and beautiful. Jacob asked Laban to give him Rachel for a wife. Laban agreed, but Jacob had to work for seven years to earn her.

At the end of seven years, Laban gave Leah, not Rachel, to Jacob. Jacob complained, but Laban explained that a younger sister cannot be married before an older sister. However, Laban told Jacob that he would give Rachel to him as well, if Jacob would first finish the wedding week celebration with Leah. At the end of that week, Laban would give Rachel to Jacob. Then Jacob would have to work another seven years. Jacob agreed.

In those days, it was legal for a man to have more than one wife. A man could also have children with the handmaids of his wives. While still living with Laban, the four women gave Jacob a total of eleven sons.

After several years, Jacob wanted to go back to his homeland. Laban said no but agreed that Jacob could have some of the sheep and goats for himself. Later, Jacob took his wives, his children, his servants, and his animals (sheep, goats, and camels) and left without telling Laban.

Jacob stopped for a short time in Bethel; see location 4 on the map. It was there that God made a covenant with Jacob and renamed him. Jacob's new name was Israel. On the way back to Hebron, Rachel gave birth to Jacob's twelfth son, Benjamin. She died in childbirth.

Finally, Jacob arrived home in Hebron. Isaac, his father, was 180 years old. Then Isaac died. By that time, Esau and Jacob had reconciled their differences. Together, they buried their father, Isaac.

G. Joseph
Genesis 37:2–50:26

Joseph was seventeen years old and was living with Jacob and his brothers in Canaan. He was his father's favorite son because he had been born in Jacob's old age. Jacob had made a special robe for Joseph, and it was thought to have many colors. Joseph's brothers hated him because his father loved him more than the others.

Joseph had a dream one night and shared it with his bothers. The dream indicated that Joseph would one day rule over his older brothers. That made the brothers hate him even more. Joseph had another dream and shared that with his brothers and his father. After that, everyone was angry at him.

One day, Joseph's brothers were tending their father's sheep. They were far from home, so Jacob sent Joseph to check on them and report back to him. Joseph had trouble finding his brothers, but a man along the way told Joseph where his brothers had gone.

When Joseph finally saw them, they were pretty far from him. The brothers saw Joseph coming and decided to make a plan to kill Joseph. However, Joseph's oldest brother, Reuben, talked the others out of killing Joseph. Instead, they took Joseph's robe from him, threw Joseph into a dry well, and left him there to die.

Then the brothers sat down to eat their lunch. As they were eating, they saw a caravan of traders passing by. The traders were on their way to Egypt to sell their merchandise. The brothers decided to sell Joseph to the traders. That way they could get money for him instead of simply letting him die. They pulled Joseph out of the cistern and sold him to the traders in the caravan. Reuben was not with them.

Later, Reuben went back to the cistern, not knowing that the other brothers had sold Joseph. When he saw that Joseph was not there, Reuben was very upset and went back to where the other brothers were.

The brothers decided to kill a goat and put the goat's blood on Joseph's robe. They took the bloody robe home with them and showed it to Jacob. They told their father that they had found the robe and thought it might be Joseph's.

Jacob said it was Joseph's robe and thought that Joseph must have been torn to pieces by a wild animal. Jacob wept bitterly.

When Joseph got to Egypt, he was placed in the home of a high official of the pharaoh (the king of Egypt). God blessed Joseph, and after a time, the official, named Potiphar, put Joseph in charge of his household and everything that he owned. Potiphar's household did very well under Joseph's care; see location 6 on the map.

Unfortunately, Potiphar's wife made advances toward Joseph. Joseph rejected her and ran from the house, but the wife claimed that Joseph had attacked her. Joseph was thrown into prison.

The prison was the one reserved for enemies of the kings of Egypt. God again blessed Joseph, and the prison warden placed all things in the prison, including the prisoners, under Joseph's care.

After a while, the cupbearer and the chief baker of the king offended Pharaoh, so Pharaoh had them both thrown into prison. The prison warden assigned them to Joseph.

One morning, when Joseph went to check on them, he noticed they both looked sad, and he asked them why. They replied that they had both had dreams during the night, but there was no one to interpret their dreams. (In those days, there were special people in the king's court who interpreted dreams.) Joseph replied that it is God who interprets dreams. He then asked the two men to tell him their dreams.

Joseph interpreted the dreams of both men. The dream of the cupbearer indicated that he would be restored to his position with the king. Joseph asked the cupbearer to say good things about him to Pharaoh when he was restored. The dream of the chief baker indicated that the king would cut off his head, and his body would be eaten by birds.

Both dreams came true. However, the cupbearer forgot to say good things about Joseph to Pharaoh.

Two years later, Pharaoh had a dream, and none of his magicians or wise men could interpret the dream. It was then that the cupbearer remembered Joseph and told Pharaoh about him. Pharaoh sent for Joseph.

Pharaoh asked Joseph to interpret the dream he had. Joseph replied,

> I cannot do it, but God will give Pharaoh the answer he desires. (Genesis 41:16 NIV)[31]

Joseph then told Pharaoh,

> It is just as I said to Pharaoh: God has shown Pharaoh what he is about to do. Seven years of great abundance are coming throughout the land of Egypt, but seven years of famine will follow them. Then all the abundance in Egypt will be forgotten, and the famine will ravage the land. The abundance in the land will not be remembered, because the famine that follows it will be so severe. The reason the dream was given to Pharaoh in two forms is that the matter has been firmly decided by God, and God will do it soon. (Genesis 41:28–32 NIV)[32]

Pharaoh put Joseph in charge of the whole land of Egypt. Joseph was thirty years old at the time. Pharaoh renamed Joseph as Zaphenath-Paneah and gave him Asenath, daughter of an Egyptian priest, to be his wife. During the seven good years, they had two sons, Manasseh and Ephraim.

Joseph organized storage areas for food during the seven years of great abundance. The food that was stored there would keep them alive during the seven years of famine.

When the good years ended and the seven years of famine began, people from other nations started going to Egypt to buy food. Jacob (Israel) sent ten of his sons (all but Benjamin) down to Egypt to buy grain. When they appeared before Joseph to ask for grain, they did not recognize Joseph. His clothes, hairstyle, and lack of beard made him look like an Egyptian, not a Hebrew.

Joseph recognized his brothers but didn't tell them who he was. The story is long but very interesting. In short, Joseph sent them home with food, but he kept one of the brothers, Simeon, and demanded that they come back a second time and bring the youngest son, Benjamin, with them.

When the brothers returned, Joseph finally revealed his real identity to them. Then he sent them back to get their father, their families, and their flocks and asked them to bring them to Egypt and spend the next five years with him. Only two years of the famine had passed at this time, and Joseph wanted to make sure they all survived.

You can see that God worked in the life of Joseph to keep Jacob and his family from dying during the famine. It also explains how Jacob, his sons, and their families came to be in Egypt.

Jacob eventually became ill and was dying. Joseph took his two sons, Manasseh and Ephraim, to see Jacob before he died. Jacob declared to Joseph that he would accept Joseph's two sons as his own sons and share, as sons, with Joseph's other brothers. Any sons born to Joseph after that day would be Joseph's sons and not considered to be a son of Jacob for inheritance purposes.

To clarify this, Jacob called all his sons together to indicate what would happen to them in the future. They were to be the twelve tribes of Israel (Jacob): Reuben, Simeon, Levi, Judah, Zebulun, Issachar, Dan, Gad, Asher, Naphtali, Joseph, and Benjamin. Manasseh and Ephraim were to be half tribes in place of Joseph, who would soon die.

Jacob's sons, including Joseph, buried him where he had asked to be buried. Then the sons who had sold Joseph into slavery were afraid that Joseph would take revenge on them. But Joseph replied,

Don't be afraid. Am I in the place of God? You intended to harm me, but God intended it for good to accomplish what is now being done, the saving of many lives. So then, don't be afraid. I will provide for you and your children. (Genesis 50:19–21 NIV)[33]

Joseph died at the age of 110. He was embalmed and laid in a casket so the Hebrews could take him to the Promised Land and bury him there when they left Egypt.

However, the Israelites remained in Egypt and eventually became enslaved as foreigners.

SECTION 6—DISCUSSION QUESTIONS

1. How can a person write, with authority, about something that happened long before that person had been born?
2. What two things did God want in His relationship with humankind?
3. Why did Adam and Eve choose to sin?
4. God was so angry and disappointed in humans that He decided to destroy all of them. However, He decided not to completely destroy humankind. Why did God change His mind?
5. God confused the languages of humankind when they were building the tower of Babel. Why were they building the tower?
6. God decided to have a nation of followers. Whom did God choose to father His nation?
7. Why did God pick this man?
8. God changed the names of two men, Abram and Jacob, in Genesis. Why?
9. Who was the man who stole his older brother's birthright? Who helped him?
10. Some men sold their younger brother into slavery. Who was the younger brother?
11. The promise of being God's nation and people was first given to Abraham. What is the relationship of the twelve sons of Jacob to Abraham?

12. Men sacrificed animals in place of themselves to pay for their sins. This manner of cleansing from sins was only temporary. This sacrifice was symbolic of another sacrifice that would be made only once. This sacrifice covered all sin, for all humankind, for all time. This "perfect" sacrifice didn't involve an animal—it involved a real man who had never sinned. Who was this man?

SECTION 7—BUILDING BLOCKS OF OUR FAITH

God's covenant with humankind is the basis for His relationship with them. He offered the relationship, so He set the rules. He pledges to love us, to care for us, and to be faithful.

What God wants in return is for us to love Him, to trust Him for our care, and to be faithful to Him. God gave us free will so that we have the option of whether we keep the covenant or not.

God initiates the process. He is always loving us, and He is always wanting love from us. He's like a brilliant light that is always shining. But we don't always look toward the light. When we think we need God, we look toward Him. The rest of the time, we look toward the darkness thinking that we can do without Him.

We should initiate, because we have a free will to do so. We should first love God with all our "heart, soul, mind, and strength" (Mark 12:30). Then God, because He loves us, will be faithful and care for us in a way that is best for us.

God has full knowledge; we don't. Therefore, we don't always recognize that what God is doing for us is the best for us. We would rather have God do for us whatever we want at the moment. But we must love Him enough to trust Him to care for us, no matter what we think.

SECTION 8—GENESIS HEADINGS

The Beginning	1:1–2:3
Adam and Eve	2:4–2:25
The Fall	3:1–3:24
Cain and Abel	4:1–4:26
From Adam to Noah	5:1–5:32
Wickedness in the World	6:1–6:8
Noah and the Flood	6:9–8:22
God's Covenant with Noah	9:1–9:17
The Sons of Noah	9:18–9:29
The Table of Nations	10:1–10:32
The Japhethites	10:2–10:5
The Hamites	10:6–1–20
The Semites	10:21–10:32
The Tower of Babel	11:1–11:9
From Shem to Abram	11:10–11:26
Abram's Family	11:27–11:32
The Call of Abram	12:1–12:9
Abram in Egypt	12:10–12:20
Abram and Lot Separate	13:1–13:18
Abram Rescues Lot	14:1–14:24
The Lord's Covenant with Abram	15:1–15:20
Hagar and Ishmael	16:1–16:16
The Covenant of Circumcision	17:1–17:27
The Three Visitors	18:1–18:15
Abraham Pleads for Sodom	18:16–18:33
Sodom and Gomorrah Destroyed	19:1–19:29
Lot and His Daughters	19:30–19:38
Abraham and Abimelek	20:1–20:18
The Birth of Isaac	21:1–21:7
Hagar and Ishmael Sent Away	21:8–21:21
The Treaty at Beersheba	21:22–21:34

A Silver Cup in a Sack	44:1–44:34
Joseph Makes Himself Known	45:1–45:28
Jacob Goes to Egypt	46:1–47:12
Joseph and the Famine	47:13–47:31
Manasseh and Ephraim	48:1–48:22
Jacob Blesses His Sons	49:1–49:28
The Death of Jacob	49:29–50:14
Joseph Reassures His Brothers	50:15–50:21
The Death of Joseph	50:22–50:26

Two Things I Will Remember About the Book of Genesis:

1. _____
   _____
2. _____
   _____

Think about what you have learned in the book of Genesis. Pick two things that you think you can easily remember and write them above. If you need a little help, read through the headings listed in section 8, or reread sections 3–7. There are no "best" answers. List what first comes to your mind. That is the information that you are most likely to remember over a long period of time.

Refer back to this page regularly to refresh your memory.

CHAPTER 2
EXODUS

In this chapter, you will get a grip on the law of God that is part of His covenant with humankind. God promises His love and care to us, but He requires love and obedience from us. The events in Exodus reveal the dilemma of humankind in their relationship with God. We agree to God's terms, we soon fall away, we suffer, we appeal to God for help, and He saves us. In Exodus, we learn of the temporary remedy for sin: confession, repentance, and sacrifice. For sacrifice to be valid, blood must be shed and life must be taken. But the cleansing is only temporary. Yet the process promises and foreshadows the permanent cleansing from our sins. That, of course, comes only through the shed blood of Jesus Christ.

Exodus is the second of the five books of the Bible referred to as the Pentateuch—Genesis, Exodus, Leviticus, Numbers, and Deuteronomy. In these books, the key idea to remember is that God is revealing Himself to His people and the laws (rules) of the relationship (covenant) between Him and them.

SECTION 1—REVIEW

In the beginning, God created everything. It was good. God and humans walked together in the cool of the evening. Humans had free will, which meant they could make their own decisions.

However, God had told humans not to eat the fruit of one tree located in the middle of the garden of Eden. That was it—just one rule, just one tree. God didn't want Adam and Eve to fail, but He knew they eventually would. We don't know how long it was before Adam and Eve failed.

God had made humans in the image or likeness of Himself. But He didn't make humans to take His place or even to be equal to Him. Neither did God make humans to be gods. The way to remember the difference is simple: God is God, and humans are not.

Because humans wanted to be like God, it was easy for Satan to tempt Adam and Eve. Satan simply asked a question that caused them to doubt God.

> Did God really say, "You must not eat from any tree in the garden?" (Genesis 3:1 NIV)[34]

Satan misrepresented what God had said. God didn't say any tree. God said not to eat from the tree of the knowledge of good and evil, because if they did, they would surely die.

Then Satan lied again when he told Eve that she would not surely die. Instead, she would become "like God, knowing good and evil" (Genesis 3:5 NIV).[35]

So humans chose to be disobedient. They believed Satan instead of God. They chose to be unfaithful to God. Humans chose to be equal with God. But of course, they weren't.

They had chosen to break the covenant (agreement) between God and humans, and that was sin! Humans rejected God instead of worshipping Him. Yet God loved His creation so much that God made clothes for Adam and Eve. Ultimately, God would give His own son for them.

As time passed, humans did many more mean and evil things. They even made false gods and worshipped them instead of God.

Finally, God was angry and decided to destroy all humankind by sending a flood. However, because God loved His creation so much, He found one man who was faithful to Him. God told that man, Noah, to build an ark. Noah, his family, and all kinds of animals were loaded on the ark and saved.

Later, God promised to create a nation of followers through one man, Abram. Abram, whom God renamed Abraham, fathered two sons; one was named Isaac. Isaac fathered two sons, one named Jacob.

Jacob, whom God renamed Israel, fathered twelve sons. When they were young men, there was a famine in their homeland, Canaan, so they moved to Egypt, where there was food. They stayed there for many years and eventually became slaves of the Egyptians.

SECTION 2—PREFACE

In Exodus, you will read about the miracles performed by God, through Moses, to persuade Pharaoh to release the Israelite slaves. You will learn more about God's love for His people as He provides food, water, and guidance on their journey out of Egypt and back toward Canaan.

You will read about God's renewed covenant with the Israelites. However, you will also read about the people's lack of trust and faithfulness toward God.

God knew this would happen, so He provided laws to help direct the people. He also provided ceremonial sacrifices to cleanse them of their sins when they broke these laws. As in Genesis, this ceremonial relief from sin was only temporary. However, it foreshadows the final, complete, lasting, perfect sacrifice of a man named Jesus, the Son of God. That sacrifice provides complete forgiveness for all our sins.

Figure 2.1 will help you track the movements of the Israelites as you learn about the book of Exodus.

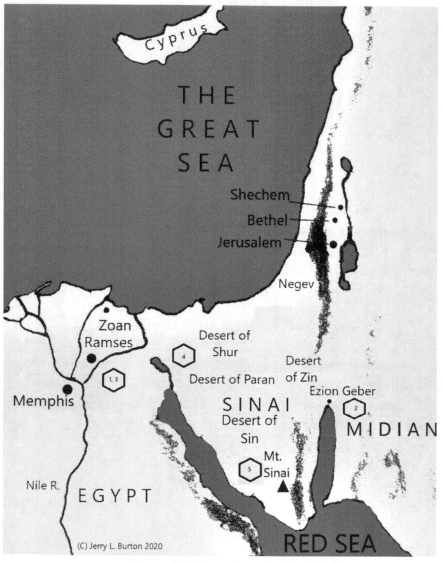

Figure 2.1. Egypt, Sinai, Midian

SECTION 3—GENERAL

Author:[36] Moses, the author of Genesis, is considered to be the author of most of Exodus.

Date Written:[37] Moses started writing Exodus in approximately 1440 BC.

Period Covered:[38] About 1805 BC (death of Joseph) through 1406 BC (death of Moses).

Audience[39]: Moses wrote Exodus for

1. the Israelites he had led out of Egypt and
2. the Israelites of future generations.

The message of Exodus is broad and includes

1. who God was;
2. how to behave toward God;
3. the wonderful things, including many wonderful miracles, done for the Israelites by God;
4. God wanting to dwell among His people; and
5. God wanting a close, loving relationship with them.

Cultural Setting:[40] In Egypt, the pharaoh was like a god to the people. Egypt also had other gods they worshipped. The Israelites had one god, Yahweh, who had miraculously helped them escape Egypt. However, the pattern of worshipping multiple gods still seemed normal to the Israelites. The long period of time the Israelites spent in the desert allowed them to change their culture of worshipping many gods to a culture that worshipped only one God.

Historical Setting:[41] Commercial routes between Egypt and Mesopotamia (present-day Iraq and Iran) and India were well developed at this time. It was not uncommon for Egypt to have many foreign people working as slaves or tenants. These foreigners could have been people who had been

1. captured during war,
2. given to Egypt as part of tribute payments,
3. victims of the slave trade, or
4. migrants looking for food and water.

Themes:[42]

1. Deliverance from the bondage of sin due to His compassionate love for humankind.
2. The covenant, which reveals the rules of God's relationship with humankind and His righteousness and other godly characteristics.
3. The tabernacle, which reveals His desire to dwell among His people.
4. Moses, God's mediator between humans and Himself, which was a foreshadowing of Jesus Christ, our mediator and redeemer.

SECTION 4—MOSES AND THE ISRAELITES IN EGYPT

A. Oppression of the Israelites in Egypt.
Exodus 1

Many years passed after Joseph had died. Eventually, Egypt had a pharaoh who had never heard of Joseph. This man began to build monuments to himself. He used innumerable slaves to do this work, and many of these slaves were Israelites—the family of Jacob.

Reference location 1 in Figure 2.1.

The population of Israelites was increasing rapidly, and Pharaoh began to worry that they might rebel and overthrow him. He made some of his own Egyptian men bosses over the Israelites. The Egyptian bosses made life very hard for the Israelite people.

The Israelites kept having children and increasing in number, so Pharaoh ordered the Israelite midwives, the women who helped pregnant women give birth to their babies, to kill all the male babies.

B. The Birth of Moses.
Exodus 2:1–10

When Moses was born, his mother, a woman of the Levite tribe, hid him for three months. Then she made a small basket and placed it in the reeds along the Nile River. The sister of Moses stood nearby to see what would happen to baby Moses.

The daughter of Pharaoh came by and stepped into the river to wash herself. She saw the basket and asked the slave girl who was standing near (Moses's sister) to get it and open it. When she opened it, Moses began to cry.

The princess felt very sorry for the baby. She saw that the baby was an Israelite child. So she asked the slave girl to find an Israelite woman to nurse the baby. The slave girl, Moses's sister, took Moses to his mother. His mother nursed and cared for Moses until he was older. No doubt he learned many stories and songs about the Israelite people from his mother.

When Moses grew older, his sister took him to Pharaoh's daughter. Pharaoh allowed his daughter to keep Moses as her son. It was Pharaoh's daughter who named the baby Moses.

Moses was raised as a member of the Egyptian royal family and received an excellent education.

C. Moses Kills an Egyptian and Runs Away.
Exodus 2:11–25

One day, after Moses became a young man, he saw an Egyptian boss beating an Israelite slave. Moses attacked the Egyptian and killed him.

When Pharaoh heard what Moses had done, he tried to kill Moses. Moses got away and went to a land called Midian.

Reference location 2 in Figure 2.1.

D. God Confronts Moses
Exodus 3:1–4:26

When Moses got to Midian, he tended the flocks for his father-in-law, Jethro. He led the flocks to the far side of the desert, to Mount Horeb, "the mountain of God." There, the angel of the Lord appeared to Moses in the flames of a burning bush.

God spoke to Moses from the bush and instructed him to go back to Egypt and tell Pharaoh to let His people go.

Moses was afraid to go back to Egypt because he knew that Pharaoh would kill him, so Moses argued with God. Here are some of the reasons Moses gave for not going back to Egypt.

1. Who am I that I should go and tell Pharaoh anything?
2. What if I go to the Israelites, and they ask me what your name is?
3. After God laid out the whole plan in detail for Moses, Moses said, "What if they don't believe me or think I am lying?" God then talked Moses through two miraculous signs to show the Israelites.

    i. God turned Moses's staff into a snake and then back into a staff again.
    ii. God turned Moses's hand leprous (diseased) and then made it clean again.

4. Finally, God told him that if the people still didn't believe him, he should take a cup of water from the Nile and pour it out on the ground. It would turn into blood.
5. Moses told God that he couldn't go speak to Pharaoh because he was slow of speech and tongue.
6. God's anger burned against Moses. But God was merciful and told Moses that his brother Aaron would speak for him.
7. Then God told Moses that the men who had wanted to kill him were dead. As a result, Moses went back to Egypt.

Reference location 3 in Figure 2.1.

E. Moses and Aaron before Pharaoh
Exodus 4:27–6:12

When Moses returned to Egypt with Aaron, the first thing they did was meet with the elders of the Israelite community and tell them what God had told Moses to do.

They answered the questions the elders had and then went to see Pharaoh. Moses and Aaron told Pharaoh that the Israelites were God's children, and God said to let them go back to Canaan.

Pharaoh laughed at Moses and Aaron and sent them away.

Pharaoh decided to punish the slaves because of Moses and Aaron. Pharaoh directed his slave drivers and foremen to tell the Israelites to collect the straw for the bricks themselves; it would no longer be provided by Egyptians. It would take the Israelites longer to make bricks because they had to collect the straw themselves. In spite of this, Pharaoh ordered them to make the same number of bricks each day as they had made before.

This made the Israelite slaves work longer and harder than before. They were very angry with Moses and Aaron.

Moses cried out to the Lord and complained. Then God said,

> Now you will see what I will do to Pharaoh: Because of my mighty hand he will let them go; because of my mighty hand, he will drive them out of his country. (Exodus 6:1 NIV)[43]

F. What God Did to Pharaoh—Persuasion by Miraculous Power
Exodus 7:8–12:30

Moses went to see Pharaoh several times before Pharaoh agreed to let the Israelites go. Here's a list of the plagues that God placed on Egypt.

1. The Plague of Blood   Exodus 7:14–24
2. The Plague of Frogs   Exodus 8:1–15
3. The Plague of Gnats   Exodus 8:16–19
4. The Plague of Flies   Exodus 8:20–32
5. The Plague on Livestock   Exodus 9:1–7
6. The Plague of Boils   Exodus 9:8–12
7. The Plague of Hail   Exodus 9:13–35
8. The Plague of Locusts   Exodus 10:1–20
9. The Plague of Darkness   Exodus 10:21–29

Some of the above plagues were directed toward one of the various gods of the Egyptians. For example, turning the Nile into blood showed God's power over the Nile, which was one of Egypt's gods.[44] The frog[45] was another god of the Egyptians. Another major god of Egypt was the bull,[46] so putting a plague on the livestock was a show of God's power over that god. The plague of darkness was showing power over the Egyptian god Ra.[47]

But Pharaoh still would not let the Israelite slaves leave Egypt. Therefore, Moses and Aaron told Pharaoh about the tenth plague, the Plague on the Firstborn (Exodus 11:1–10). This final plague would demonstrate God's power over all life. This was God's way of showing Pharaoh that the God of Moses was greater than all the gods of Egypt.

Moses and Aaron announced to Pharaoh that God had proclaimed,

> About midnight I will go throughout Egypt. Every firstborn son in Egypt will die, from the firstborn son of Pharaoh, who sits on the throne, to the firstborn son of the slave girl, who is at her hand mill, and all the firstborn of the cattle as well. (Exodus 11:4–5 NIV)[48]

Pharaoh refused to believe Moses and Aaron, and he sent them away.

God gave Moses a list of things to do in order to keep the plague from affecting the Israelites. Following these instructions caused the death angel to pass over the homes of the Israelites who had followed the instructions.

This wonderful yet terrifying event is still celebrated today as the Passover. It includes a festival called the Festival of Unleavened Bread.

The Israelites had to hurry to prepare the meal required for the Passover, so they didn't have time to wait for the bread to rise. Leaven, or yeast, is what causes bread to rise. But because they didn't have time to let it rise, they made the bread without leaven—unleavened bread. This story is in Exodus 12:1–30.

Here are the instructions that Moses gave to the Israelites.

The Israelites were told to kill a male goat or lamb and spread some of its blood on the top and sides of the door frame of the home. Then, they were to cook and eat the meat. All of it had to be consumed. If any was left, it had to be burned. God ordered that this event be remembered and celebrated every year.

SECTION 5—THE GREAT ESCAPE

A. The Escape
Exodus 12:31–14:31

During the night, thousands in Egypt died. Pharaoh's son was one of them. Pharaoh called Moses and Aaron in and said,

> Up! Leave my people, you and the Israelites! Go, worship the LORD as you have requested. Take your flocks and herds, as you have said, and go. And also bless me. (Exodus 12:31–32 NIV)[49]

The Israelites had already gathered their belongings and were ready to go. There were about six hundred thousand men, not counting women and children. The men were dressed for battle.

Earlier, the Israelites had gone to their Egyptian neighbors and asked for articles of silver and gold. Many of the Egyptians liked the Israelites and were willing to help them.

The Israelites had lived in Egypt for 430 years, to the day, when they left. God went before them in a pillar of cloud during the day and in a pillar of fire during the night.

When Pharaoh was told that the Israelites had left, he changed his mind about them going. He suddenly realized that he had let much of his workforce leave. He took all the chariots of Egypt, with officers over all of them. He also took horsemen and troops and chased after them. He caught up to the Israelites in camp at the sea.

Location 4 in Figure 2.1 may be close to where the Israelites had made camp. Therefore, it may be where the Red Sea parted.

The Israelites looked up and saw the Egyptian army approaching them. The people were filled with fear and were angry with Moses for getting them to leave Egypt.

Moses told them to stand firm, and the Lord would deliver them. The angel of God (in the cloud) left the front of the Israelites and moved to the rear, between the two armies. The Egyptians stopped advancing and held their ground.

During the last watch of the night, the cloud brought darkness to one side and light to the other so that neither side attacked the other during that time.

God caused the wind to blow all night and parted the waters so the Israelites could cross to the other side.

The Egyptians tried to follow the Israelites, but God caused confusion in the army. Wheels came off of the chariots, and they weren't able to follow quickly.

When the Egyptian army was finally able to get to the water and start crossing behind the Israelites, the wind stopped, and the waters returned to their original position, drowning the entire Egyptian army.

Once again, God saved His people.

B. Wandering in the Desert
Exodus 15–40

The Israelites were in the desert for forty years before entering the Promised Land. During this time, God performed many miracles to save the Israelites from death. They could have died of thirst, starvation, disease, or snakebite.

Each time the Israelites moved from one place to another, they had to tear down camp before leaving and then set it up again when they arrived at a new campsite. They moved only when the cloud or pillar of fire moved.

SECTION 6—THE GIVING OF THE LAW: THE TEN COMMANDMENTS

A. At the Foot of Mount Sinai
Exodus 19:1–25

Reference location 5 in Figure 2.1.

Three months after leaving Egypt, the Israelites came to the Desert of Sinai. They camped in front of the mountain.

God told Moses to go up the mountain. From the top of the mountain, God told Moses to tell the people the following.

1. You saw what I did to Egypt and how I saved you from the Egyptians.

2. If you will obey Me and keep My covenant, then you will receive favor from Me.
3. The whole world is Mine, and I will make you a kingdom of priests and a holy nation.

God wanted the nation of Israel to love Him and obey Him. In turn, God would care for and bless the nation of Israel. When other nations saw this relationship between God and His nation, Israel, those other nations would want to serve the God of the Israelites too.

When Moses told the people all that God had said, they agreed to make the covenant with God. Then Moses took the people to the foot of the mountain, where they could hear God speaking to him and to them.

B. The Ten Commandments
Exodus 20:1–17

God spoke the Ten Commandments to the Israelite people as they gathered at the foot of the mountain.

1. I am the LORD your God, who brought you out of Egypt, out of the land of slavery. You shall have no other gods before me.
2. You shall not make for yourself an image in the form of anything in heaven above or on the earth beneath or in the waters below. You shall not bow down to them or worship them; for I, the LORD your God, am a jealous God, punishing the children for the sin of the parents to the third and fourth generation of those who hate me, but showing love to a thousand generations of those who love me and keep my commandments.
3. You shall not misuse the name of the LORD your God, for the LORD will not hold anyone guiltless who misuses his name.
4. Remember the Sabbath day by keeping it holy. Six days you shall labor and do all your work, but the

seventh day is a sabbath to the LORD your God. On it you shall not do any work, neither you, nor your son or daughter, nor your male or female servant, nor your animals, nor any foreigner residing in your towns. For in six days the LORD made the heavens and the earth, the sea, and all that is in them, but he rested on the seventh day. Therefore the LORD blessed the Sabbath day and made it holy.

5. Honor your father and your mother, so that you may live long in the land the LORD your God is giving you.
6. You shall not murder.
7. You shall not commit adultery.
8. You shall not steal.
9. You shall not give false testimony against your neighbor.
10. You shall not covet your neighbor's house. You shall not covet your neighbor's wife, or his male or female servant, his ox or donkey, or anything that belongs to your neighbor. (Exodus 20:2–17 NIV)[50]

C. Structure of the Ten Commandments—Please Remember

1. The first four commandments are about your relationship with God.
2. The last six commandments are about your relationship with other people.

D. Try to memorize some form of the following condensed version of the Ten Commandments:

1. I am the Lord your God; you will have no other gods before me.
2. Do not make or worship any images that are man-made.
3. Do not use the name of the Lord in reference to anything but the Lord.
4. Keep the Lord's day holy.

5. Treat your mother and your father with respect.
6. Do not kill.
7. Do not cheat on your husband or wife.
8. Do not steal.
9. Do not lie.
10. Do not long for anything that belongs to another person.

E. Moses Receives Instructions Concerning Laws and Procedures
Exodus 20:22–24:3

After God had spoken the Ten Commandments at the foot of Mount Sinai, the people remained at a distance while Moses approached the thick darkness where God was. There, God gave many more instructions to Moses concerning laws and procedures.

Then Moses returned to the people and told them what God had said, and they agreed to all of it.

SECTION 7—THE GOLDEN CALF

A. Moses Returns to the Mountain to Receive the Ten Commandments in Stone
Exodus 24:9–31:18

God told Moses to come back up the mountain and to bring with him the seventy elders (leaders) of the Israelites. Moses did as God had told him. After the elders had seen God and had lunch, they went back down the mountain.

Moses and Joshua, Moses's assistant, went higher up the mountain with God. They stayed on top of the mountain with God for forty days and forty nights.

B. Aaron Makes a Golden Calf
Exodus 32:1–35

The Israelites in camp began to believe that something had happened to Moses and that he was not coming back. The people went to Aaron and said,

> Come make us gods who will go before us. As for this fellow Moses who brought us up out of Egypt, we don't know what has happened to him. (Exodus 32:1 NIV)[51]

The people brought all their gold earrings to Aaron. Aaron fashioned all the gold into an idol in the shape of a calf. The people saw the idol and liked it. Remember that one of the gods of Egypt was a bull.

Aaron then built a stone altar in front of the golden calf. The next day, the people rose early, sacrificed burnt offerings, and presented fellowship offerings. Afterward, they sat down to eat and drink and celebrate.

Up on the mountain, the Lord told Moses what Aaron and the people were doing. God was so angry that He thought about destroying all of them except Moses. Moses asked God not to destroy them, and God agreed not to. Moses, in approaching God this way, was acting as a mediator. A mediator is one who presents a positive case for someone else. That is what Jesus does for us: He is our mediator between us and God.

Then Moses picked up the two tablets. He and Joshua headed back down the mountain. Before they even got down from the mountain, they could hear the noise of the camp celebrating around the golden calf.

When Moses got close to the camp and saw the calf and the people celebrating. He was so angry that he threw the tablets down and broke them into pieces.

Moses took the calf and burned it. Then he ground it into a fine powder, scattered it on the water, and made the people drink it.

Moses asked God to forgive the people for what they had done, and God said that He would. However, He also said that they had to be punished. Then the LORD sent a plague upon the people.

C. God Makes Two More Tablets for Moses
Exodus 34:1–38

The LORD said to Moses,

> Chisel out two stone tablets like the first ones, and I will write on them the words that were on the first tablets, which you broke. (Exodus 34:1 NIV)[52]

This verse always makes me chuckle—the part where God says "which you broke."

SECTION 8—THE TENT OF MEETING AND THE TABERNACLE EXODUS 33:7–40:38

God, starting in Exodus 26, had given very specific instructions for the building of a sacred area called the tabernacle. Several places in Exodus describe the furniture, the priestly clothes, the altars, and more that should be used in the tabernacle.

In chapter 33, the tent of meeting, the place where God would meet with Moses, was set up outside the camp. It may be that God was still angry with the people because of the golden calf and refused to go inside the camp.[53]

Whenever Moses went out to the tent, all the people would rise and stand at the entrances to their tents. They would worship as Moses entered the tent. As Moses went into the tent, the pillar of cloud would come down. The cloud would stay at the entrance for as long as the LORD was speaking with Moses.

Inside the tent, the LORD would speak to Moses face-to-face, like friends would do. When all was said and done, the cloud would lift, and Moses would leave the tent and return to the camp. Joshua, Moses's young aide, would stay at the tent. It is generally thought that Joshua kept watch at the Tent of Meeting except when he accompanied Moses up Mount Sinai. Moses was about eighty years old when the Israelites left Egypt. Joshua died just sixteen years after Moses. We don't know when Joshua was born. *Young* as used in Exodus 33:11 might be a relative age, and Joshua may have been in his twenties or older at the time.

Take a moment to reflect on the mental picture you were asked to create with God, Adam, Eve, and you standing together and making conversation.

In the last chapter of Exodus, God tells Moses to set up the tabernacle.

Figure 2.2. The Tabernacle[54]

The tabernacle was a rectangular area. The area was "fenced off" by cloth panels. Inside the paneled area were the various pieces of furniture and equipment God had specified. There was a tent at the far end of the tabernacle; that was the tent of meeting (the holy place).

Inside the tent of meeting, at the far end, was a small room behind curtains. This area was the "holy of holies." When God was in the holy of holies, the room was filled by the cloud of the presence of God. The cloud of God's presence rose from a piece of "furniture" called the ark of the covenant. This was a very important piece of furniture.

The ark of the covenant, like every other part of the tabernacle, was defined in detail by God. Before the ark of the covenant was placed inside the tent of meeting, the two tablets on which the law was written were placed inside the ark. The ark was like a box or chest, and inside it was the covenant, the agreement between God and the Israelites. That is why it is called the ark of the covenant. It was kept in the holy of holies at all times, except when the camp was moving.

Ultimately, the ark would be moved into the temple in Jerusalem. But Jerusalem did not yet belong to the Israelites.

SECTION 9—DISCUSSION QUESTIONS

1. Moses asked God the following three questions. How did God answer these three questions?
   a. Who am I that I should go and tell Pharaoh anything?
   b. What if I go to the Israelites, and they ask me what your name is?
   c. What if they don't believe me or think I am lying?
2. Why did God give the law to the Israelites?
3. Could the Ten Commandments be thought of as a summary of the law?
4. What is a miracle?
5. Do you think you would have responded to God like Moses when God told him to return to Egypt? Why or why not?

6. What has the law got to do with the culture of the nation of Israel?
7. What influence did the religions of the surrounding nations have on the religious beliefs of the Israelites?
8. What influences of our culture do you see in our religious practices?
9. The plagues in Egypt were primarily aimed at the Egyptian deities. How many Egyptian deities can you associate with the plagues God sent on Egypt?
10. How did the religious culture under Yahweh differ from the religious culture of Egypt?
11. Just for fun, read Exodus 34:29–35, "The Radiant Face of Moses."
    a. Tell the story aloud, as best as you can remember.
    b. Next, write it down as if you were writing it in a letter to a friend.

SECTION 10—BUILDING BLOCKS OF OUR FAITH

God has revealed much about who He is and what He does. I am fascinated with Exodus 34:5–7. In fact, I find the ease with which the Almighty describes Himself almost amusing.

> Then the LORD came down in the cloud and stood there with him and proclaimed his name, the LORD. And he passed in front of Moses, proclaiming, "The LORD, the LORD, the compassionate and gracious God, slow to anger, abounding in love and faithfulness, maintaining love to thousands, and forgiving wickedness, rebellion and sin. Yet he does not leave the guilty unpunished; he punishes the children and their children for the sin of the parents to the third and fourth generation." (Exodus 34:5–7 NIV)[55]

God reveals Himself as

1. the Lord;
2. compassionate;

3. gracious;
4. slow to anger;
5. abounding in love and faithfulness;
6. maintaining love to thousands;
7. forgiving wickedness, rebellion and sin; and
8. not leaving the guilty unpunished.

Beyond that, God even appears to the people and dwells with them in the tabernacle.

It is clear from the law that we cannot satisfy the requirements of the covenant. We need a mediator to go before God on our behalf, as Moses did for the Israelites. But even Moses could not convince God to forgive some of the sins of the people. At this point, in the Old Testament, there seems to be no hope for the salvation of humankind.

We will learn soon that there is a mediator for us. A man, God in the flesh, named Jesus who mediates for us. It is through Him that the penalty for our sins has been paid.

But we still have more to learn about the holiness of God and the seriousness of the covenant between Him and ourselves.

In Leviticus, the next book in our study, God establishes guidelines for the priesthood. The priests have a major role in helping the people keep their part of the covenant with God. They also served as mediators for humankind.

SECTION 11—EXODUS HEADINGS

The Israelites Oppressed	1:1–1:22
The Birth of Moses	2:1–2:10
Moses Flees to Midian	2:11–2:25
Moses and the Burning Bush	3:1–3:22
Signs for Moses	4:1–4:17

The Tabernacle	36:8–36:38
The Ark	37:1–37:9
The Table	37:10–37:16
The Lampstand	37:17–37:24
The Altar of Incense	37:25–37:29
The Altar of Burnt Offering	38:1–38:7
The Basin for Washing	38:8
The Courtyard	38:9–38:20
The Materials Used	38:21–38:31
The Priestly Garments	39:1
The Ephod	39:2–39:7
The Breastpiece	39:8–39:21
Other Priestly Garments	39:22–39:31
Moses Inspects the Tabernacle	39:32–39:43
Setting Up the Tabernacle	40:1–40:33
The Glory of the Lord	40:34–40:38

Two Things I Will Remember About the Book of Exodus:

1. _____
   _____
2. _____
   _____

Think about what you have learned in the book of Exodus. Pick two things that you think you can easily remember and write them above. If you need a little help, read through the headings listed in section 11, or reread sections 3–10. There are no "best" answers. List what first comes to your mind. That is the information that you are most likely to remember over a long period of time.

Refer back to this page regularly to refresh your memory.

CHAPTER 3
LEVITICUS

In this chapter, you will get a grip on the righteousness demanded by God. The demand is so great that one entire tribe of Israel, the Levites, is set aside to serve as priests. They do it right, or they die. The book of Leviticus can be thought of as an instruction manual for the Levites.

Leviticus is the third of the five books of the Bible referred to as the Pentateuch: Genesis, Exodus, Leviticus, Numbers, and Deuteronomy. In these books, the key idea to remember is that God is revealing Himself to His people and the law (rules) of the relationship between Him and them.

Before we get into Leviticus, let's do a little review.

SECTION 1—REVIEW

In Exodus, we learned the following.

1. God revealed His ability and willingness to break the natural laws (laws of nature), and He often does so for the purpose of helping His people. This is called performing a miracle. God performed many miracles to help his people throughout the book of Exodus. He also broke some laws of nature to punish them.

2. God spoke the Ten Commandments directly to the Hebrew people. However, it scared them so badly that they asked Moses to be their mediator. A mediator is one who is a go-between. That is, God would speak to Moses, and then Moses would tell the people what God had said. It also worked the other way: the people would speak to Moses, and he would speak to God for them. Today, Jesus is our mediator. That is why we pray "in Jesus's name."

3. God allowed Moses and the seventy elders to go up the mountain and see God. They even ate and drank in His presence. However, God required that all the people who went up the mountain had to be cleaned in a "blood anointing" ceremony before coming into the presence of God. The event was one example of ceremonial cleansing. God told Moses to send the elders back to camp and come further up the mountain to receive the Ten Commandments on two stone tablets.

4. Moses remained on the mountain for forty days. After forty days, Moses returned down the mountain with the two stone tablets. He saw the people worshipping the golden calf and threw the stone tablets to the ground, breaking them into pieces.

5. Eventually, God called Moses back up the mountain to receive a second set of tablets. When Moses came down and Aaron and the people saw him, they were afraid because Moses's face was glowing. Moses had to cover his face with a veil. He removed the veil only when he was speaking to God.

6. By the end of Exodus, the tabernacle had been completed, inspected by Moses, and filled with the Presence of God (Exodus 40:34).

SECTION 2—PREFACE

In Leviticus, you will read more about God's holiness and how important it is to God's identity, integrity, and authority. God's holiness is also critical to a clear understanding and full appreciation of the price Christ paid for our unholiness.

You will also learn more about biblical sin and how it affects your relationship with God. You've already learned that ceremonial sacrifice was a temporary remedy for sin, yet it played a major role in healing the broken relationship between humankind and God in the Old Testament.

However, in Leviticus, you will learn that only when executed perfectly—in the right place, in the right way, by the right person, and with the right intent—could the ceremony be effective. That is why a priesthood, the Levites, was established to conduct all the ceremonial sacrifices. Leviticus is the instruction manual for the Levitical priesthood.

An important thing to remember as you read through Leviticus is that these ceremonial sacrifices and the perfection required were only a foreshadowing of the perfect sacrifice that removes our sin completely and forever. That perfect sacrifice of a lamb without blemish was, of course, the crucifixion of Jesus, the Christ.

Finally, you will understand the importance of worship.

SECTION 3—GENERAL

Figure 3.1. Israelites at Mt. Sinai

Author:[56] Moses is considered to be the author of most of Leviticus. According to Leviticus 27:34, Moses was told by God to write Leviticus.

Date Written:[57] Moses started writing Leviticus around 1440 BC. The Israelites were still near Mount Sinai. Reference location 1 in Figure 3.1.

Period Covered:[58] Between 1446 BC and 1406 BC.

Audience:[59] The original intent was probably that the primary audience would be the Israelite priests and Levites who administered worship, sacrifices, and the law. Later on, lay people also became familiar with the book, but the Levites were still responsible for maintaining the integrity of the law.

Cultural Setting:[60] The book of Leviticus contains the system of laws administered by the Levites. The Levites were one of the twelve tribes of Israel (twelve sons of Jacob). The twelve tribes, called the Hebrew nation, were required by God to live in accordance with all the laws given by Him. The Levites were set aside for priestly service to the nation. They owned no land, and they were supported by the tithes of the rest of the Hebrews.

The Levitical Priesthood:[61] Leviticus means "pertaining to Levites." Moses and Aaron were Levites. Moses was God's leader for the Hebrews. Aaron's family was set apart to become priests. The other Levites were assistants to the priests.

Historical Setting:[62] The book of Leviticus picks up where the book of Exodus left off. The tabernacle had been built.

The major empires in the Middle East at that time were Egypt and Mesopotamia (modern-day Iraq). Everything in between was an area of small centers of population referred to as city-states.[63]

SECTION 4—THE LAW AND
THE HOLINESS OF GOD

In Exodus, the law was given. The administration of the civil laws had been delegated in Exodus to a system of Judges. Now, in the book of Leviticus, the system for the administration of the spiritual side of the law—offerings and sacrifices and feasts—had to be established. The holiness of God was communicated clearly in the law. But now, God's holiness had to be reflected in the administration of the law.

A set of procedures was established by God, through Moses, for each type of sacrifice and for the celebration of festival days.

The major Old Testament sacrifices can be grouped into two categories: voluntary and mandatory.[64]

Voluntary sacrifices are generally acts of worship. These would include burnt offerings, grain offerings, and fellowship offerings.

Mandatory sacrifices are associated with atonement for sin. These include sin offerings and guilt offerings.

A. Voluntary Sacrifice Procedures

Each sacrifice had a very specific set of requirements. The requirements were so specific that one can almost think of them as a script for a play. There are specific acts that must be performed by specific individuals. These acts must be performed at a specific location, usually relative to the Altar or entrance to the tent of meeting. These acts also must be performed in a specific sequence.

To illustrate this, I've detailed the procedures for the burnt offering. The scriptural reference for this is Leviticus 1:1–17.

1. **The Burnt Offering**
   a. Order of ceremony if the animal was from a herd (Leviticus 1:1–9).
      i. The giver had to select a male (bull) without defect.
      ii. The giver then had to present it at the entrance to the tent of meeting.
      iii. There, the giver had to lay his hand on the head of the animal being offered; in this way, the offering became acceptable to the Lord on behalf of the giver.
      iv. The giver slaughtered the animal before the Lord.

v. Next, the blood of the slaughtered offering was splashed on the sides of the altar at the entrance of the tent of meeting. This was done by Aaron's sons, the priests.

vi. Meanwhile, the giver skinned the animal and cut it into pieces.

vii. Aaron's sons put fire on the altar and arranged the wood. Then, the priests arranged all of the cut pieces of offering, including the head and fat, on the burning wood.

viii. The internal organs and the legs of the animal were washed in water by the priests and burned on the altar as well.

b. Order of ceremony if the animal was from a flock (Leviticus 1:10–13).

i. The giver had to select a male (sheep or goat) without defect.

ii. The giver then took it to the north side of the altar, where he slaughtered it before the Lord.

iii. The priests splashed the blood of the animal against the sides of the altar.

iv. The giver then cut the animal into pieces, including the head and fat, which the priests arranged on the burning wood.

v. The giver washed the internal organs and the legs and gave them to a priest, who took them to the altar and burned them.

c. Order of ceremony if the offering was birds (Leviticus 1:14–17).

i. The giver had to bring a dove or a young pigeon.

ii. The priest was the one who took the offering to the altar. Then he wrung the head off of the bird and burned it on the altar.

iii. The priest drained the blood on the side of the altar.

iv. The priest removed the feathers and the crop and discarded them to the east of the altar, where the ashes were.

> v. The priest then tore the bird open by the wings, being careful not to divide it completely. Then he burned it on the altar.

Notice the level of detail in the procedures of these offerings to the Lord.

Why was it important to follow the procedures exactly?

God is righteous and holy and cannot be in the presence of sin or imperfection. God would not accept anything that was not perfect. If the procedure was not done properly, God would not honor it.

In chapter 10 of Leviticus, we are given an example of how serious God is about His holiness being observed.

2. The Death of Nadab and Abihu (Leviticus 10:1–2)

Aaron and his sons (Eleazar, Ithamar, Nadab, and Abihu) had been ordained as priests in chapter 8. The ceremony involved a sin offering and a series of burnt offerings.

After the ordination of Aaron and his sons, they began to minister to the people in chapter 9. Aaron conducted a sin offering and a burnt offering for himself. Then he officiated sin offerings, burnt offerings, and fellowship offerings for the Israelites.

Moses and Aaron went into the tent of meeting. When they came out, they blessed the people. Then, the glory of the Lord appeared to the people, and the offering on the altar was consumed by fire that came out of the presence of the Lord.

In chapter 10, two of Aaron's sons, Nadab and Abihu, in preparation for an offering ceremony, put fire in their censers and added incense. Then Nadab and Abihu offered it before the Lord, but they had not followed the proper protocol. Apparently, the fire they put in the censers did not originate from the correct place. This meant that the fire was unauthorized and therefore unacceptable. Entering the holy place with anything unacceptable would defile the holy place—the holy place would become unholy. To prevent this from happening, fire came out of the presence of the Lord and it consumed and killed Nadab and Abihu.[65]

In Leviticus, God says,

> Be holy because I, the LORD your God, am holy. (Leviticus 19:2 NIV)[66]

This statement is the main message of the book of Leviticus—that God is holy, and we must also be holy.

What does holy mean, and why is holiness important?

Most definitions of biblical holiness include the idea of separateness. It means anyone who is holy is separate or set aside—for example, a holy man, a priest, a rabbi, the people of God, et cetera. Another characteristic often mentioned when defining biblical holiness is the idea of perfection, or being worthy of worship and recognition.

The Lord, then, is holy in the biblical sense. God is set aside. There's only one God worthy of being worshipped. He is good and righteous. He is also the God of love.

When God tells us that we should be holy because He is holy, He is telling us to be sinless and that our actions should be different from those who are sinful.

There is a short statement in one of my favorite Bibles, the NIV Cultural Backgrounds Study Bible, which simplifies this idea of holiness.

> Holiness distinguishes God from people and God's people from other people.[67]

B. Mandatory Sacrifice Procedures

Adam and Eve chose to be unrighteous and unholy. They sinned. In doing so, through them, sin entered the world and affected us all.

Sin is doing anything that God says is wrong. Sin is also failing to do anything that God says we should do. Even the "smallest" sin will separate us from God—for eternity. Only God has the ability to change that result. The good news is that God, the source of the law that condemns us, is also the one who can wash us clean of our sin.

The offerings and sacrifices of Leviticus do not offer a one-time, permanent solution to our sinful condition.

Leviticus discusses the two ceremonial remedies for sin. These two ceremonial sacrifices are the sin offering and the guilt offering. We'll take a quick look at the sin offering.

1. The Sin Offering

> For the life of a creature is in the blood, and I have
> given it to you to make atonement for yourselves on the
> altar; it is the blood that makes atonement for one's life.
> (Leviticus 17:11 NIV)[68]

There are several scenarios that require a sin offering. For example, in one case, it might be an anointed priest who has unintentionally committed a sin. In that case, the sin offering would be conducted as follows.

a. The priest would bring a young bull without defect.
b. The priest would present it at the entrance to the tent of meeting.
c. The priest would then lay his hand upon the head of the bull and slaughter it.
d. Then the priest would take some of the bull's blood and carry it into the tent of meeting.

e. There, the priest would dip his finger in the blood and sprinkle some of it seven times in front of the curtain of the sanctuary.

f. Next, the priest would put some of the blood on the horns of the altar of fragrant incense.

g. The priest would pour out the remaining blood at the base of the altar for burnt offerings.

h. After that, the priest would remove all the fat, including any fat attached to internal organs, and burn it on the altar of burnt offerings.

i. The remains of the bull (hide, head, legs, flesh, and internal organs) would be removed from the camp and taken to the ceremonially clean place, where the ashes were thrown. There, it would be burned on a wood fire on the ash heap.

Some of the other scenarios requiring a sin offering were

a. if the whole Israelite community had sinned unintentionally,

b. if a leader had sinned unintentionally, or

c. if an individual member of the community had sinned unintentionally.

The service would differ slightly for each of the above situations. The animal being offered might be different, the person offering the animal could be different, and the role of the priest could also vary.

C. Satisfying the Law and God's Holiness

> Sacrifice is a mechanism to pray to God, thank God, preserve sacred space for God, and be in a relationship with God.[69]

Sacrifices provided only temporary atonement, but they also provided a visual, active picture of the process of redemption. Notice the requirements.

1. Acknowledgement of sin.

2. Desire to be washed clean of the sin.

3. An innocent and perfect stand-in for the sinner. Blood had to be shed; a life had to be taken. It was a price that had to be paid and should have been paid by the sinner.
4. A mediator, the priest, who presents the sacrifice to God.

For Christians, Jesus is both the mediator and the perfect sacrifice. Christ paid the price that you and I should pay. By the grace of God, we are forgiven.

Grace will be discussed in detail in a later chapter. For now, you need to understand that grace is not mercy. Mercy would be God giving a punishment that is less than what a person should receive. Grace is receiving no punishment at all for our sin because the price has already been paid by Jesus.

SECTION 5—WORSHIP

Leviticus reveals God's desire to be present with His people and to enjoy fellowship with them. From the very beginning, God created humans in His own image, and He wanted them to have a close, loving, intimate relationship with Him—a father-child type relationship. If you remember from our study of Genesis, before the fall of man, God walked with Adam in the garden in the cool of the evening (Genesis 3:8). Sin broke that relationship.

If God is righteous and holy (i.e., "perfect" and "set apart") and cannot be in the presence of sin or imperfection, can we ever experience a close, warm, and loving relationship with God?

The answer to that question is yes! Because God is gracious and loving, He made a covenant with humans. God will love us, and we must love Him. There are two ways in which God measures our love for Him:

1. by our obedience to His commands, and
2. by our worship of Him.

In Exodus, God complains to Moses because some of the people went out to gather food on the Sabbath.

> How long will you refuse to keep my commands and my instructions? (Exodus 16:28 NIV)[70]

God closes the Fourth Commandment with,

> but showing love to a thousand generations of those who love me and keep my commandments. (Exodus 20:6 NIV)[71]

This is even reflected by Jesus in the New Testament when He says,

> If you love me, keep my commandments. (John 14:15 NIV)[72]

We also show love for God by worshipping Him. Our worship, because we have free will, brings glory to God. Isaiah, one of the prophets you will study in another book, says,

> I will say to the north, "Give them up!" and to the south, "Do not hold them back!" Bring my sons from afar and my daughters from the ends of the earth—everyone who is called by my name, whom I created for my glory, whom I formed and made. (Isaiah 43:6–7 NIV)[73]

Notice the phrase "whom I created for my glory." We were created to bring glory to God. Worshipping God is a very strong way of giving God glory. When we acknowledge things that God has done for us, it brings Him glory. When we speak of God to other people, it brings God glory. All these things are a form of worship!

The *Cambridge Dictionary* defines worship as "to have or show a strong feeling of respect and admiration for God or a god."

In Leviticus, the people worshipped God by giving Him offerings.

There are many different types of sacrifices and offerings mentioned in Leviticus, but one of the most common offerings was the burnt offering, described in Leviticus 1:1–17. It is described as "a food offering, an aroma pleasing to the LORD."[74]

The burnt offering was common back in Genesis and Exodus. It was an offering given by humans to please God. It was a form of worship and praise.

There is another common offering referred to as the fellowship offering. Another name for it is the well-being offering. This offering is given for the same reason as the burnt offering—that is, to praise God and to improve our relationship with God.

We don't really give offerings like this in our country, but people in some other countries still do. There are many ways we can give offerings that please God.

1. Give money to a church or religious organization.
2. Give money, food, clothes, etc. to needy organizations or individuals.
3. Volunteer our time to work for a church or other religious cause.
4. Give our time to help others do things that they can't do for themselves—"love your neighbor as yourself."
5. Serve in a ministry—singing in the choir, greeting people at church, cleaning the church, and many more church-related tasks.
6. Give to or serving in secular organizations as part of your Christian witness of love for God and your neighbor.

All these offerings are pleasing to God and fall into a large category called worship because we are doing these things to please God. In addition, even by ourselves, we can worship God. We can sing praises to Him as we work or play, and we can talk to Him any time of day or night.

When we talk to God, we don't have to think of it as prayer. It's simply talking with God. What do we say to God? You say whatever is on your mind or in your heart. God wants to hear you say it with your lips, with your voice, and from your heart. That is sweet praise to God.

Too often, we think talking to God is simply asking Him for things. Although there is a place and time for that, Jesus gives us a proper format for prayer. It's called the Lord's Prayer.

> This, then, is how you should pray:
> "Our Father in heaven,
> hallowed be your name,
> your kingdom come,
> your will be done,
> on earth as it is in heaven.
> Give us today our daily bread.
> And forgive us our debts,
> as we also have forgiven our debtors.
> And lead us not into temptation,
> but deliver us from the evil one." (Matthew 6:9–13 NIV)[75]

Notice and remember that the prayer begins by acknowledging, or recognizing, who God is. God is the Almighty, and He is in heaven. Hallowed means He is very highly respected. He obviously is a king—the king. We acknowledge that His kingdom will come and His will is going to be done, and we should want it that way. After we acknowledge God and who He is, Jesus says we can make our requests known.

God is very pleased when He hears us acknowledge who He is. In fact, God describes Himself as

> The LORD, the LORD, the compassionate and gracious God, slow to anger, abounding in love and faithfulness, maintaining love to thousands, and forgiving wickedness, rebellion and sin. (Exodus 34:6–7 NIV)[76]

These are great things to tell God He is. That is acknowledging Him, praising Him and worshipping Him. This brings, or adds, glory to God.

It's a wonderful thing to do to start the day, it's a wonderful thing to do throughout the day, and it's a wonderful thing to do at the end of the day! You will be amazed at how personal your relationship with God will become!

In short, worship is acknowledging who God is and what He has done by expressing your love, honor, thanks, and praise to Him. Reading God's Word is another way of worshipping and praising God. When I read scripture, I read it to God, as if He and I were discussing it. Often I read it aloud to God.

One last thing: When you spend time with God, try to remember how Moses and God spoke in the tent of meeting.

> The LORD would speak to Moses face to face, as one speaks to a friend. (Exodus 33:11 NIV)[77]

Like a good friend, be sure to listen. It should be a two-way conversation. How do you listen?

> Be still, and know that I am God. (Psalm 46:10 NIV)[78]

Worship is a wonderful beginning to an intimate relationship with God. Worship also sustains that intimacy.

SECTION 6—DISCUSSION QUESTIONS

1. How would you describe God's holiness?
2. What is sin? What problem does it cause?
3. What is a ceremonial sacrifice?
4. What is the difference between a ceremonial sacrifice and Christ being crucified?
5. What is worship?

SECTION 7—LEVITICUS HEADINGS

The Burnt Offering	1:1–1:17
The Grain Offering	2:1–2:16
The Fellowship Offering	3:1–3:17
The Sin Offering	4:1–5:13
The Guilt Offering	5:14–6:7
The Burnt Offering	6:8–6:13
The Grain Offering	6:14–6:23
The Sin Offering	6:24–6:30
The Guilt Offering	7:1–7:10
The Fellowship Offering	7:11–7:21
Eating Fat and Blood Forbidden	7:22–7:27
The Priests' Share	7:28–7:38
The Ordination of Aaron and His Sons	8:1–8:36
The Priests Begin Their Ministry	9:1–9:24
The Death of Nadab and Abihu	10:1–10:20
Clean and Unclean Food	11:1–11:47
Purification After Childbirth	12:1–12:8
Regulations about Defiling Skin Diseases	13:1–13:46
Regulations about Defiling Molds	13:47–13:59
Cleansing from Defiling Skin Diseases	14:1–14:32
Cleansing from Defiling Molds	14:33–14:57
Discharges Causing Uncleanness	15:1–15:33
The Day of Atonement	16:1–16:34
Eating Blood Forbidden	17:1–17:16
Unlawful Sexual Relations	18:1–18:30
Various Laws	19:1–19:37
Punishments for Sin	20:1–20:27
Rules for Priests	21:1–22:16
Unacceptable Sacrifices	22:17–22:33
The Appointed Festivals	23:1–23:2
The Sabbath	23:3

The Passover and Festival of Unleavened Bread	23:4–23:8
Offering the First Fruits	23:9–23:14
The Festival of Weeks	23:15–23:22
The Festival of Trumpets	23:23–23:25
The Day of Atonement	23:26–23:32
The Festival of Tabernacles	23:33–23:44
Olive Oil and Bread Set before the Lord	24:1–24:9
A Blasphemer Put to Death	24:10–24:23
The Sabbath Year	25:1–25:7
The Year of Jubilee	25:8–25:54
Reward for Obedience	26:1–26:13
Punishment for Disobedience	26:14–26:46
Redeeming What Is the LORD's	27:1–27:34

Two Things I Will Remember About the Book of Leviticus:

1. _____
   _____
2. _____
   _____

Think about what you have learned in the book of Leviticus. Pick two things that you think you can easily remember and write them above. If you need a little help, read through the headings listed in section 7, or reread sections 3–6. There are no "best" answers. List what first comes to your mind. That is the information that you are most likely to remember over a long period of time.

Refer back to this page regularly to refresh your memory.

CHAPTER 4

NUMBERS

In this chapter, you will get a grip on the importance of trusting in God. Numbers is the fourth of five books of the Bible referred to as the Pentateuch: Genesis, Exodus, Leviticus, Numbers, and Deuteronomy. In these books, the key idea to remember is that God is revealing Himself to His people and the rules of the relationship between Him and them.

Before we get into Numbers, let's do a little review.

SECTION 1—REVIEW

In the book of Leviticus, we should have learned the following.

1. God is holy, consecrated, set apart, and righteous. He is without sin or fault and makes no mistakes. He has authority over all things. He is the God Almighty.
2. Sin is anything against God's will. The effect of sin is that it breaks our relationship with God. The penalty for sin is death with the shedding of blood.
3. In the Old Testament, ceremonial sacrifices fall into two categories: voluntary and mandatory.
    a. Voluntary sacrifices are generally
        i.   expressions of worship;
        ii. atonement for unintentional sin in general;
        iii. expression of devotion, commitment, and complete surrender to God;

    iv. recognition of God's goodness and provisions; and/or

    v. thanksgiving and fellowship.

  b. Mandatory sacrifices are generally related to atonement for sin.

4. Jesus is both the mediator and the perfect sacrifice.

5. Sin separates us from God and has caused us to have to experience a physical death. Without removal of sin, we would die and be eternally separated from God. Sacrifices were a temporary fix in the Old Testament, but the New Testament presents Jesus, the Son of God, as the permanent fix for our sin problem.

6. Worship and praise, acknowledging who and what God is, allow us to enjoy His presence, His love, and His guidance in this life. Because of Christ, we have the Holy Spirit of God present in us to help us and to bear witness to our redemption. Praise God! Talk to God often and remember to spend time listening to Him.

SECTION 2—PREFACE

In reading Numbers, you will begin to recognize that the Israelites started coming together like a nation. By this time, they had moved from the area of Mount Sinai, location 1 in Figure 4.1, to an area bordering on the Promised Land, location 2, the plains of Moab.

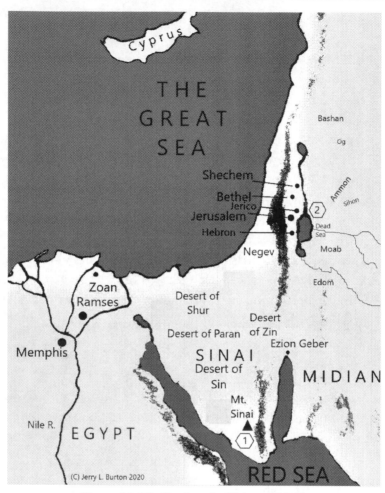

Figure 4.1. Mt. Sinai to the Plains of Moab

God, through Moses, organized His nation by assigning various levels of judges and military leaders within each tribe. Then, He began to prepare them for entry into Canaan. However, several things happened that displeased God, and the entry into Canaan was postponed.

God's fatherly love for the Israelite nation continued to be demonstrated as seen in Genesis, Exodus, and Leviticus. God rewarded obedience but punished disobedience. Even Moses was punished for disobeying God.

Of all the Israelites who escaped from Egypt, only Caleb and Joshua were allowed to enter the Promised Land. They had faith that, with God, Canaan could have been taken.

As you read, you should appreciate more fully

1. the presence of God in the pillar of cloud and the pillar of fire;
2. the reasons for each census;
3. the worship value of the ark of the covenant;
4. the seriousness of the covenant between God and humankind; and
5. the degree to which God wants to have a strong, intimate relationship with humankind.

SECTION 3—GENERAL

Author:[79] Moses is considered to be the author of most of Numbers. It's assumed that Moses is being assisted by scribes. The scribes typically take down information word for word as they are told. The substance of the message would have come from Moses. It is probable that some portions, like the following verse, were added by someone else.

> Now Moses was a very humble man, more humble than anyone else on the face of the earth. (Numbers 12:3 NIV)[80]

Date Written:[81] Moses probably started writing Numbers during the period 1440 BC to 1400 BC.

Period Covered:[82] Between 1445 BC and 1406 BC. Numbers tells us what was happening during the move from the wilderness near Mount Sinai to the plains of Moab, on the border of the Promised Land.

Audience:[83] Israelites who survived the period from the exodus through the giving of the law and the migration to Moab for the purpose of entering the Promised Land (Canaan). This group included the "second" generation who would have used this writing for cultural and historical guidance.

Cultural Setting:[84] By this time, the Israelites had developed an identity as a nation under God and were subject to the laws of God and the covenant with God. The Hebrew name for this book is *bemidbar*, which means "in the desert."

Historical Setting:[85] Middle or latter part of the Late Bronze Age. During this period of time, Egypt was the dominant power in the region—including the land of Canaan. In general, the Egyptian focus was on maintaining commercial trade routes through northern Sinai and into Canaan. This resulted in the Israelites being able to move into Canaan without having to confront the Egyptians.

SECTION 4—NUMBERS

A. The First Census
Numbers 1:1–54

A census of the Israelites was taken while they were still at Mount Sinai. They were preparing to start their journey from Mount Sinai toward the Promised Land. The census included only names of men twenty years and older. These men were organized to fight in the army and were listed by divisions.

The actual count is uncertain. There are at least two different approaches to determining the census count.[86] But with God on their side, the numbers didn't really matter.

It was important to know the military strength of the Israelites, but there was another reason for taking a census. The census determined how many people were in each tribe. This was important because when they got to the Promised Land, each tribe would receive a share of land proportional to the size of their tribe.

Each tribe of Jacob (one for each of his twelve sons) had its own area in the camp. In place of Joseph, there were two tribes: Ephraim and Manasseh, the two sons of Joseph.

The tribe of Levi was camped in the center of the campsite. They were divided into three small groups: Merari, Gershon, and Kohath. The tribe of Levi represented the priesthood. They would not be given their own land in the Promised Land; instead, the priests would live among the other tribes.

There was one other small group in the center area. That group included Moses and the active priests.

In the very center of all the groups was the tabernacle. In the tabernacle was the tent of meeting.

In the diagram of the camp arrangement, the numbers in parentheses are numbers representing the approximate population of each tribe.

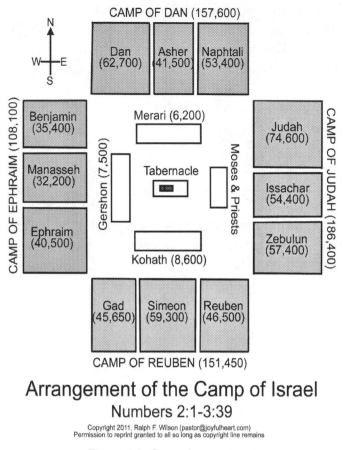

CAMP OF DAN (157,600)

CAMP OF EPHRAIM (108,100)

CAMP OF JUDAH (186,400)

CAMP OF REUBEN (151,450)

Arrangement of the Camp of Israel
Numbers 2:1-3:39

Copyright 2011, Ralph F. Wilson (pastor@joyfulheart.com)
Permission to reprint granted to all so long as copyright line remains

Figure 4.2. Camp Arrangement

Notice that Judah was the largest tribe and therefore would receive the greatest amount of land. Benjamin was the smallest and would receive the least amount of land.

B. God Shows Love for His Nation and His Wrath for Disobedience

God showed His love for the Israelite nation by continuing to dwell among them. God's presence in the tabernacle was shown by the cloud that was over the tabernacle. During the day, the cloud covered the tabernacle. During the night, the cloud appeared as a cloud of fire.

God also showed His love for the Israelite nation by continuing to guide them on their journey from Egypt to the plains of Moab. As long as the cloud remained over the tabernacle, the Israelites remained camped where they were. However, when the cloud moved up, away from the tabernacle, the Israelites broke camp and followed the cloud.

God showed His love for His people not only by guiding them along the way but also by providing sustenance for them. God supplied food (manna) and water (from dew) to the people.

C. The Israelites Leave Sinai
Numbers 10:11–11:34

As the Israelites traveled toward the Desert of Paran, close to the Promised Land, there were many hard times. Often, the Israelites would complain and rebel against Moses and God. One source even refers to the book of Numbers as "the Book of Complaining"![87]

For example, after a while, the people got tired of eating manna and complained. They wanted meat to eat. It angered God. The next day, God caused a wind to start blowing quail in from the sea. When it stopped, the quail were piled up three feet high for as far out from camp as a day's walk. At first this seemed like a blessing, but what happened next was more like a plague or curse.

God was still angry with the people for complaining, so He caused the meat to turn rotten while it was still in their teeth. All the people who had asked for meat instead of the manna died and were buried there.

There were other rebellions along the way. But finally, the Israelites reached the Desert of Paran. There, they camped.

D. Exploring Canaan
Numbers 13:1–14:25

The time had come for the nation of Israel to enter the Promised

Land. The land was already occupied by the Canaanites, so battles would have to be fought. God told Moses to pick a leader from each of the twelve tribes. Moses sent the twelve men into Canaan to spy on the people and the land.

The spies were to determine whether the people in Canaan looked healthy and strong, whether the land looked good for grazing animals, whether the soil was good for growing food, and whether their cities were walled.

The Israelite spies were gone for forty days before they returned. When they got back to the Israelite camp, the entire nation was called together to hear what the spies had found out. This is the account given to Moses.

> We went into the land to which you sent us, and it does flow with milk and honey! Here is its fruit. But the people who live there are powerful, and the cities are fortified and very large. (Numbers 13:27–28 NIV)[88]

Then, they told the nation more about the people who they saw in Canaan and where the different groups of people lived.

Caleb, a leader and spy from the tribe of Judah, silenced everyone and said,

> We should go up and take possession of the land, for we can certainly do it. (Numbers 13:30 NIV)[89]

The other spies argued that the people in the land were too large and strong for Israel.

Then, all the people in the camp except Caleb and Joshua rebelled against Moses and Aaron. Joshua was a young man and the spy from the tribe of Ephraim. Caleb and Joshua spoke to the whole assembly of Israelites, saying,

The land we passed through and explored is exceedingly good. If the LORD is pleased with us, He will lead us into that land, a land flowing with milk and honey, and will give it to us. Only do not rebel against the LORD. And do not be afraid of the people of the land, because we will swallow them up. Their protection is gone, but the LORD is with us. Do not be afraid of them. (Numbers 14:7–9 NIV)[90]

The whole assembly talked about stoning Caleb, Joshua, and Moses. But then the glory of the Lord appeared at the tent of meeting where all could see it!

God was very angry with the Israelites and ready to destroy them, but Moses appealed to God, reminding Him of what He had said about Himself on Mount Sinai.

The LORD is slow to anger, abounding in love and forgiving sin and rebellion. Yet He does not leave the guilty unpunished; He punishes the children for the sins of the fathers to the third and fourth generation. (Numbers 14:18 NIV)[91]

The Lord forgave them, but because the Israelites did not trust God to help them, He declared that none of the men who had seen the miracles in Egypt and in the desert would live to enter the Promised Land—except for Caleb and Joshua.

God told Moses to break camp the next morning and set out toward the desert along the route back to the Red Sea.

Ten of the twelve spies (not Caleb and Joshua) were struck down with a plague and died.

Then Moses told the people they were headed back toward the Red Sea. Many of the men realized that they had sinned by not relying on the Lord. They now believed that if they attacked the Canaanites, God would help them, and they would succeed. Moses told them it was too late, and God had said they must leave. But they disobeyed God again, this time by attacking the Canaanites. God did not help them, and they were beaten back into the desert.

God had made it clear that the Israelites would wander in the desert for the next forty years. By the end of those forty years, all the men who had been twenty years or older at the time of the census would be dead except for Caleb and Joshua.

E. Korah, Dathan, and Abiram
Numbers 16:1–50

There were many arguments and uprisings against Moses during the thirty-nine years before the Israelites were allowed to go back to Moab and enter the Promised Land. Because the people continued to sin against God, the Lord told Moses to have everyone put tassels on the corners of the clothes. Hopefully, the tassels would help them remember to obey God's laws.

Three men, Korah, Dathan, and Abiram, were very upset because they thought they were holy enough to not be corrected by Moses. They gathered the support of 250 Israelite leaders and went to talk with Moses and Aaron. They told Moses and Aaron that they believed the whole community was holy, and the group felt that Moses and Aaron thought they were better than everyone else.

Moses told the men and all their followers to come back the next day, and they all would appear before the Lord. Aaron would appear with them, and the Lord would decide who was holy and who was not.

The next day, everyone except Korah, Dathan, and Abiram gathered at the entrance to the tent of meeting. The glory of the Lord appeared.

The Lord told Moses and Aaron to move away from all the others so He could destroy them. Moses and Aaron cried out to God and asked Him not to destroy the whole assembly just because one man had sinned. In this case, it was actually three men who had sinned by leading the rebellion.

God told Moses to tell the other people to move away from the tents of Korah, Dathan, and Abiram.

When everyone had moved away from the tents, the wives and children of Dathan and Abiram came out and stood at the doors to their tents. Korah stood at the door of his tent too.

Then Moses said,

> This is how you will know that the LORD has sent me to do all these things and that it was not my idea: If these men die a natural death and experience only what usually happens to men, then the LORD has not sent me. But if the LORD brings about something totally new, and the earth opens its mouth and swallows them, with everything that belongs to them, and they go down alive into the grave, then you will know that these men have treated the LORD with contempt.
>
> As soon as he finished saying all this, the ground under them split apart and the earth opened its mouth and swallowed them, with their households and all Korah's men and all their possessions. They went down alive into the grave, with everything they owned; the earth closed over them, and they perished and were gone from the community. (Numbers 16:28–33 NIV)[92]

Then, fire came out from the Lord and consumed the 250 men who had supported Korah in his rebellion against Moses and Aaron.

There is more to this story. Numbers 16:36–50 tells you the rest. I encourage you to take a little time to read it.

When we read stories like this, it's easy to jump to the conclusion that God is hateful and full of wrath. But what we have to remember is that God is holy and righteous. We are neither holy nor righteous, but through His mercy and grace, we are alive! The fact that we are alive and God gives us mercy and grace demonstrates that His love for us is greater than His wrath.

In fact, His love for us is so much greater for us than His wrath that He gave His Son to die in our place as a perfect sacrifice for the removal of all our sins. This act of God is called grace. He removes our sins, even though we are not worthy.

F. The Budding of Aaron's Staff
Numbers 17:1–13

The Israelites were still mad at Moses and Aaron, so the Lord instructed Moses to have the leader of each tribe bring his staff to him.

The name of each leader was placed on his personal staff. Aaron's name was placed on the staff from the tribe of Levi. The staffs were placed in the tent of meeting in front of the testimony.

Then Moses told them that God would make the staff of His chosen leader bloom, and God expected the rebellions to end.

The next day, when Moses entered the tent to check on the condition of each staff, he had a surprise. He brought all the staffs out for the people to see for themselves. Not only had Aaron's staff budded, but it had blossomed and produced almonds!

Each man, except Aaron, took back his staff.

The Lord told Moses to put Aaron's staff in front of the testimony, to be kept there as a sign against rebellion.

Ultimately, the staff was placed in the ark of the covenant, along with the two tablets with the Ten Commandments on them and a jar of manna.

Contents of the Ark of the Covenant

1. The Ten Commandments   Exodus 25:16, 21
2. Aaron's rod   Numbers 17:10
3. A jar of manna   Exodus 16:31–34

G. Water from the Rock
Numbers 20:1–13

Another interesting story about things that happened during the forty years of wandering involved Moses striking a rock in order to get water for the Israelites.

This story comes from a time when the Israelites were in the Desert of Zin. There was no water in the area, and the Israelites, as they had done so many times before, complained against Moses and Aaron, saying they wished they were back in Egypt as slaves because at least they would have food and water.

Moses and Aaron went to the tent of meeting, where the glory of the Lord appeared to them. The Lord told Moses to take Aaron and get all the people together in front of a certain rock. There, Moses was to speak to the rock, and water would pour out of it.

Moses and Aaron did as God had said and gathered the people in front of the rock. Then Moses said,

> Listen, you rebels, must we bring you water out of this rock? (Numbers 20:10 NIV)[93]

Then Moses raised his arm and struck the rock twice with his staff. Water gushed out, and the community and their livestock drank.

But the Lord was extremely displeased with Moses and Aaron and told them that neither of them would be allowed to bring the people into the Promised Land.

Can you identify what Moses and Aaron did that was wrong?

Moses's words made it sound like he and Aaron had made the water come out of the rock. If Moses and Aaron had made the water come out of the rock, this miracle of God would have been viewed as magic being performed by Moses and Aaron. That would indicate that Moses and Aaron had Godlike powers.

But the greater wrong was that Moses had not trusted God to do the work that God said He would do. In addition, Moses did not speak to the rock, as he was instructed to. Instead, Moses struck the rock with the "magic" staff. For a moment, it seems that Moses may have assumed himself to be equal with God.[94]

H. The Death of Aaron
Numbers 20:22–29

God instructed Moses to take Aaron and his son, Eleazar, to the top of Mount Hor. God also revealed to Moses that Aaron would die there. When Moses took Aaron to the mountain, he removed Aaron's priestly clothes and put them on Eleazar, Aaron's son. Then Aaron died on top of Mount Hor.

I. The Bronze Snake
Numbers 21:4–9

The people had wanted to take a shortcut through a land called Edom to get to the Promised Land. Edom told them no, so the Israelites had to travel back along the route to the Red Sea.

Once again, the people began to speak against God and Moses. The people had manna and water, but they complained that they didn't like the manna. In fact, they even said that they detested it.

Therefore, God sent poisonous snakes among them. The snakes bit the people, and the people began to die.

The pattern of behavior was repeating itself. The people promised to obey, they disobeyed, they got punished, and finally they cried out to Moses to ask God to get rid of the snakes.

Of course, Moses prayed for the people. Then God, in His love and mercy, told Moses to make a snake and put it up on a pole. Moses did as God told him.

The people were told that if they were bitten by a snake, they should look at the snake on the pole, and they would be healed.

God's "snake on a pole" and the modern medical symbol of the World Health Organization are very similar.

In some ancient Near East cultures, it was not uncommon to ward off causes of harm by displaying images of them as protection against them. Snakes were a very common threat.[95]

Jesus said, according to the Gospel of John,

> Just as Moses lifted up the snake in the wilderness, so the Son of Man must be lifted up, that everyone who believes may have eternal life in him. (John 3:14–15 NIV)[96]

J. Balaam's Donkey
Numbers 22:21–23:12

This is a fun story, and it begins in Numbers 21:21. The Israelites wanted to pass through the land of the Amorites on their way to the plains of Moab, across the Jordan from Jericho. They offered to stay on the highway. Yes, it was a heavily traveled main road. They promised not go into any of the fields or use any of the water.

The king of the Amorites, King Sihon, denied passage to the Israelites and sent his whole army out to confront them. That was a big mistake. Israel conquered his army, killed him, and took much of his land. In Figure 4.3, King Sihon's land is east of the number 1.

Figure 4.3. Kingdoms of Sihon and Og

Then, the Israelites went up the road toward Bashan. The king of Bashan, Og, also met the Israelites with his entire army. The Israelites killed the king, his sons, and his entire army. The Israelites left no survivors. They also took his land that was north of the number 1 in Figure 4.3.

As Numbers 23 begins, the Israelites had reached and entered the plains of Moab. They made camp along the Jordan River just across from Jericho.

The king of Moab was a man named Balak. Balak had seen what Israel had done to the Amorites when they had tried to attack the Israelites, and Balak was terrified. He was afraid that if he let the Israelites pass through his land, they would ruin it because there were so many of them.

Balak decided to ask a diviner for advice. Should he simply ignore the Israelites and let them pass, or should he attack them?

A diviner is a person who would talk to a deity for another person. In this case, that other person was Balak. When the diviner received an answer from the deity, he would send that answer back to the person who had asked the question. There was usually a fee charged for the divining service.

Balak chose to deal with a diviner named Balaam. Balaam was famous, but he was not a prophet of Yahweh. He was known by many of the countries in the Middle East. His nonbiblical prophecies are recorded in Aramaic text dating back to 700 BC.[97]

Balak sent messengers, along with the fee for divination, to seek Balaam's help. In his message, Balak told Balaam that a huge mass of people had come out of Egypt and settled near him. These people from Egypt were more powerful than he and his army were. Balak asked Balaam to put a curse on them so he could defeat them in battle and drive them from his country. Balak ended his message with a statement of confidence, saying that he knew that Balaam's blessings and curses worked.

When the messengers spoke to Balaam, Balaam told them to spend the night there, and in the morning, he would give them the answer he received from the Lord.

During that night, God came to Balaam and spoke to him. Balaam told God that the men who had come to him were from the king of Moab, Balak, and that they had asked him to put a curse on the Israelites.

God told Balaam not to go back with these men to their country. He also said not to put a curse on the Israelites because they were blessed.

The next morning, Balaam told Balak's princes (messengers) to go back to their own country without him because the Lord refused to let him go.

Balak's messengers went back and reported to Balak that Balaam would not come.

Balak then sent more men and higher ranking officials to see Balaam. They told Balaam that he would be handsomely rewarded if he went back with them.

Balaam's answer was that even if Balak gave him his entire palace filled with gold and silver, Balaam could not do any more than what God would allow him to do. But then he told the messengers to stay there that night, and he would inquire again to see what the Lord would allow him to do.

Sure enough, that night, God came to Balaam, but this time God told Balaam to go ahead and go with Balak's princes. But God didn't really want him to go.

The next morning, Balaam got up, saddled his donkey, and rode off with Balak's princes. What Balaam didn't know was that God had sent the angel of the Lord to stand in the road and block the way.

Balaam wasn't able to see the angel standing in the road and holding a drawn sword, but the donkey could see it! The poor little donkey ran off the road into a field. Balaam, still on the donkey, started beating her to get her back on the road.

The angel of the Lord then stood in a narrow path between two vineyards. There were walls on both sides of the path. The donkey tried to run around the angel. As she ran close to the wall, she crushed Balaam's foot, and of course, Balaam beat her again.

The angel of the Lord moved a little way up the road to a place that was so narrow, one could not even turn to the side, either to the left or to the right.

This time, when the poor donkey saw the angel of the Lord, she lay down under Balaam. Balaam was extremely angry and began to beat the donkey.

Then the Lord opened the little donkey's mouth. She spoke to Balaam and asked him why he had beaten her these three times.

Balaam told the donkey that she had made a fool of him and that if he had a sword, he'd kill her!

The donkey answered that she had always been his donkey and had seldom done this kind of thing to him.

Balaam agreed that she didn't usually act this way.

Finally, the Lord opened Balaam's eyes so that he could see the angel. When Balaam saw the angel standing in the road with his sword drawn, he bowed low and fell face down.

The angel then spoke to Balaam and explained that the donkey had seen him and tried to avoid him. The angel told Balaam that if the donkey had not turned away, he would have killed Balaam and spared the donkey.

Balaam acknowledged his sin and asked the angel what he should do.

The angel of the Lord told him to go ahead and go with the men but to speak only what he was told to speak.

Balaam continued on and met with Balak.

There is more to the story, but I suggest you read the rest on your own.

K. The Second Census
Numbers 26:1–65

While in Moab, the Israelite men began joining the Moabite women in the ceremonies of the pagan god of Moab, the Baal of Peor. These actions resulted in a plague among the Israelites. Many people died, so God ordered another census taken.

L. The Transjordan Tribes[98, 99]
Numbers 32:1–42

At the end of the forty years in the wilderness, the Israelites began to move back toward the plains of Moab. On their way, they passed through regions occupied by the Edomites, Moabites, Ammonites, Amorites, and other tribes. There were no military confrontations with the Edomites, Moabites, or Ammonites at first. However, as you may remember from the story of Balaam's donkey, the kings of the Amorites and of Bashan were a different story.

The Amorite king, Sihon, had extended his realm into the northern half of Moab. He refused to grant passage to the Israelites as they went through Moab. When King Sihon attacked Israel, his troops were defeated, and he was killed. Israel took control of his territory, and it became the inheritance to the tribe of Reuben.

The king of Bashan, Og, was concerned about the advancement of the Israelite army northward after the defeat of King Sihon. Og's troops attacked the Israelites, and again the Israelites prevailed.

Now, the Israelites had captured all the territory on the east side of the Jordan from the Arnon River in Central Moab to Mount Hermon at the northern extent of Bashan. All the Transjordan territory was allotted to Reuben, as noted before, as well as Gad and East Manasseh.

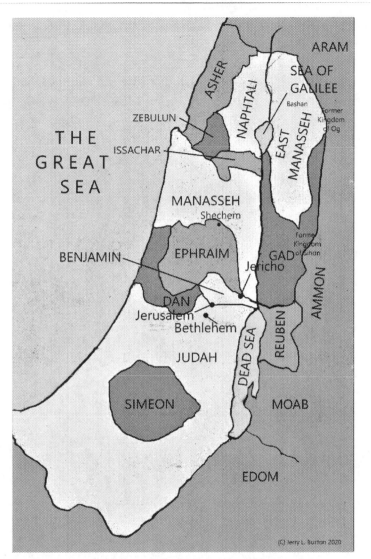

Figure 4.4. Defeat of the Kingdoms of Sihon and Og

M. Moses Gives Final Instructions to the Israelites

In the remainder of the book of Numbers, Moses organized the Israelites and assigned the land in Canaan to the various tribes. Each of the tribes told the Levites in which towns they could live. The boundaries were set for each tribe, and the tribes were responsible for taking their land away from the Canaanites.

Everything was set for the invasion of Canaan and the taking of the Promised Land. The only thing left was for Moses to renew the covenant between God and the Israelites, bless the people, and die.

SECTION 5—DISCUSSION QUESTIONS

1. Why was it necessary to take a census? Discuss two reasons for doing this.
2. What happened when the Israelites asked for meat to eat?
3. What did Moses do that displeased God?
4. How many spies went into Canaan, and how long did they stay?
5. Who were the two spies who trusted God to help if the Israelites invaded Canaan?
6. What happened to the ten spies who didn't trust God?
7. What happened to Korah and his two fellow leaders, Dathan and Abiram?
8. What happened to the 250 leaders who considered themselves holy and offered incense to God?
9. What are the contents of the ark of the covenant?
10. The bronze snake on a pole foreshadows what person?
11. Why was a second census required?
12. What tribes settled in the Transjordan territory?

SECTION 6—NUMBERS HEADINGS

The Census	1:1–1:54
The Arrangement of the Tribal Camps	2:1–2:34
The Levites	3:1–3:51
The Kohathites	4:1–4:20
The Gershonites	4:21–4:28
The Merarites	4:29–4:33
The Numbering of the Levite Clans	4:34–4:49
The Purity of the Camp	5:1–5:4
Restitution for Wrongs	5:5–5:10
The Test for an Unfaithful Wife	5:11–5:31
The Nazirite	6:1–6:21
The Priestly Blessing	6:22–6:27
Offerings at the Dedication of the Tabernacle	7:1–7:89
Setting Up the Lamps	8:1–8:4
The Setting Apart of the Levites	8:5–8:26
The Passover	9:1–9:14
The Cloud above the Tabernacle	9:15–9:23
The Silver Trumpets	10:1–10:10
The Israelites Leave Sinai	10:11–10:36
Fire from the Lord	11:1–11:3
Quail from the Lord	11:4–11:35
Miriam and Aaron Oppose Moses	12:1–12:16
Exploring Canaan	13:1–13:25
Report on the Exploration	13:26–13:33
The People Rebel	14:1–14:45
Supplementary Offerings	15:1–15:21
Offerings for Unintentional Sins	15:22–15:31
The Sabbath Breaker Put to Death	15:32–15:36
Tassels on Garments	15:37–15:41
Korah, Dathan, and Abiram	16:1–16:50
The Budding of Aaron's Staff	17:1–17:13

The Transjordan Tribes	32:1–32:42
Stages in Israel's Journey	33:1–33:56
Boundaries of Canaan	34:1–34:29
Towns for the Levites	35:1–35:5
Cities of Refuge	35:6–35:34
Inheritance of Zelophehad's Daughters	36:1–36:13

Two Things I Will Remember About the Book of Numbers:

1. _____
   _____

2. _____
   _____

Think about what you have learned in the book of Numbers. Pick two things that you think you can easily remember and write them above. If you need a little help, read through the headings listed in section 6, or reread sections 3–5. There are no "best" answers. List what first comes to your mind. That is the information that you are most likely to remember over a long period of time.

Refer back to this page regularly to refresh your memory.

✡ ✡ ✡

CHAPTER 5
DEUTERONOMY

In this chapter, you will get a grip on the process the Israelites had to go through before being allowed to enter the Promised Land. You will also see the nation of Israel on the verge of total success, only to settle for a compromise of what God had called them to.

Deuteronomy is the last of five books of the Bible referred to as the Pentateuch: Genesis, Exodus, Leviticus, Numbers, and Deuteronomy. In these books, the key idea to remember is that God is revealing Himself to His people and the laws (rules) of the relationship between Him and them.

Before we get into Deuteronomy, let's do a little review.

SECTION 1—REVIEW

The first four books of the Pentateuch (Genesis, Exodus, Leviticus, and Numbers) show us that God's creation was an act of great love. Everything He created was "good, very good." In fact, it was perfect. God walked and talked with humans for some undefined period of time. God loved humankind, and in return, humankind loved God. God took care of humankind. They were given only one rule, but they were also given a free will—they could choose to do whatever they wanted to do. And they chose to break the one rule God had given them.

Even after humans sinned, God took care of them. However, when humans acquired the knowledge of good and evil, God had to define what was allowed and what was not. Because God is perfect, He requires perfection around Him. Humans were no longer perfect, so the former relationship was lost.

In order for God and humankind to continue a close relationship, one where God lives in the presence of humans and takes care of them, humans would have to be sinless or somehow have their sins forgiven. Forgiveness could only come after the price of sin was paid. The price of sin, as God had warned humankind, is death.

For God to forgive sin, He had to set up a system of sacrifices and offerings. He instructed Moses to have priests perform these sacrifices and offerings. There were strict rules about sacrifices and offerings and how they had to be done. If they were done wrong, God wouldn't accept them.

The sacrifice for removal of sin required the shedding of blood and the death of the man, but God allowed the priest to substitute an animal for the man. However, the sacrifice only covered the sins already committed. When a man sinned again, there had to be another sacrifice for the removal of his sin.

As you may remember, Moses led God's people, the Israelites, out of slavery in Egypt. This was another example of God's great love for His people. After God had given the law to Moses at Mount Sinai, God led them toward the Promised Land.

When the Israelites were close to the Promised Land, they sent spies into Canaan (the Promised Land) to see how hard it would be to defeat the people there. After forty days in Canaan, the spies came back and reported what they had seen to the rest of the Israelites. Ten of the spies were very negative and thought the Israelites would surely be defeated if they invaded Canaan. However, one of the spies, Caleb, said that with God, the victory would be won. The twelfth spy, Joshua, agreed with Caleb. The Israelites chose to not trust God and rebelled against Moses, Caleb, and Joshua.

Because of their rebellion, God led them back into the wilderness, where they would spend forty years, one year for each of the days the spies spent in Canaan. During that time, those who had rebelled would die because they had not trusted God to defeat the Canaanites.

At the end of the forty years, God led the Israelites back toward Canaan. Moses, Caleb, and Joshua were the only Israelites from forty years ago who were still alive. Now, the Israelite nation was made up of the children and grandchildren of the original group from Egypt. They had a large number of men of military age. None of these people had been slaves in Egypt.

No one in this new generation had formally agreed to the rules for having a personal relationship with God (the covenant). Now, with the "new" Israelite nation in position to enter the Promised Land, Moses needed to define the covenant with God for the new generation and have them make a commitment to keep the covenant.

SECTION 2—PREFACE

Deuteronomy is the final account of the nation of Israel before it crossed the Jordan into the Promised Land. Before any of the Israelites could go into the Promised Land, they had to renew the agreement between the people of the nation and God. This agreement was mentioned numerous times in the preceding books. It is called the covenant.

The ark of the covenant was the ark that God had told Moses to build. The ark contained the two tablets with the Ten Commandments inscribed on them by the finger of God, Aaron's rod which had budded, and a jar of manna to remind the people that God had provided for them in the desert. The ark was kept in the holy of holies in the tabernacle except when Israel was changing locations or going into battle. Then, it had to be carried by the priests in front of the procession.

The Israelites had gathered in Moab, near Mount Nebo.

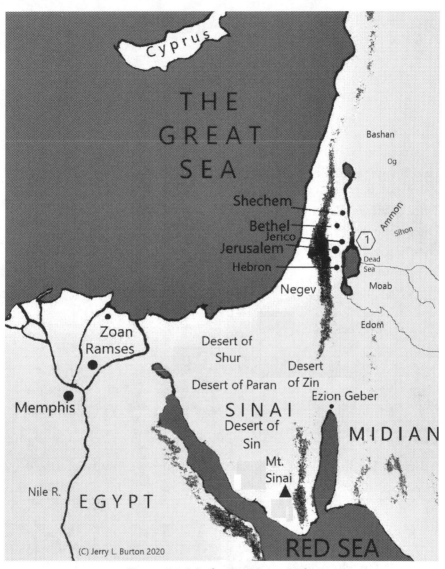

Figure 5.1. Moab near Mount Nebo

From there, the plan was that they would proceed across the Jordan River and into Canaan. Because Moses had failed God, he would die before that happened. Joshua, Moses's assistant, would be the one to lead Israel into the Promised Land.

Moses presented the contents of the book of Deuteronomy in three separate speeches. Most of this information had been given to the Israelites before.

SECTION 3—GENERAL

Author:[100] Moses is considered to be the author of most of Deuteronomy. The book begins with a preamble that may have been written by someone else. It ends with the death and burial of Moses.

Date Written: It's hard to date the actual writing of the book of Deuteronomy. Certainly, most of the content came from Moses. Some chapters, such as chapters 32 and 33, may have been delivered orally and later recorded in written form.[101] One source indicates that the written book may not have appeared until approximately 1400 BC.[102]

Period Covered:[103] Between 1446 BC and 1406 BC.

Audience:[104] The original audience was the generation of Israelites who were either very young when they left Egypt, or who were born after their parents left Egypt. Future generations would also read this book and see it as the book of the law.[105]

Cultural Setting[106]: The new nation of Israel was well organized by now. Each tribe had judges and military leaders. The Israelites with Moses now were not the Israelites who had left Egypt with Moses. Much of the Egyptian culture had been transformed to a new, nationalistic, monotheistic culture. It was important for this new generation to know its roots. Therefore, it was necessary for Moses to explain to these new Israelites who they were, how they ended up in Moab, and where they were going.

Historical Setting:[107] Israel's military weapons were inferior to the greatest powers in the region, but Egypt was weakening and no longer making incursions into Canaan. The other power in the region was Mesopotamia. However, they had not yet taken advantage of the diminished strength of Egypt. This meant that the people in Canaan had to face the invasion by the Israelites without help from any outside power.

The events of Deuteronomy took place in the territory of Moab near where the Jordan River flows into the Dead Sea.

Main Theme:[108] The central theme in Deuteronomy is the covenant relationship between humans and God. This relationship began when God called Abraham to love and serve Him as the one true God. In return, God promised to make a great nation of believers out of Abraham's descendants and to bless and care for them.

The covenant was passed from Abraham to Isaac, then from Isaac to Jacob. The seed of Jacob then blossomed into the twelve tribes of Israel. Each tribe was descended from one of the twelve sons of Jacob.

After living in Egypt for about 430 years (Exodus 12:40–41), the culture of the Hebrews had undoubtedly shifted toward Egyptian culture in many ways. The Egyptians had their own belief system that involved numerous gods. The covenant made between God and humans had not been forgotten by the Hebrews, but it probably was not at the core of their culture.

God used Moses to return the people to a culture whose belief system was centered on the covenant made by God with Abraham, Isaac, and Jacob.

After the exodus generation failed to trust God and enter the Promised Land, their sons and daughters who had been less influenced by the Egyptian culture had their chance. They had lived thirty-nine more years in a culture that was centered in love for, and dependence upon, an almighty and faithful God.

But even they, people with a free will, were subject to rebellion.

Ultimately, in Deuteronomy 29, the people are told that if they are to enter the Promised Land, they must agree to the covenant.

SECTION 4—DEUTERONOMY

It had been forty years since Moses had led the people out of Egypt. God spoke to Moses and told him it was time to move toward Canaan, so they broke camp and travelled to Moab.

They made camp just east of the Jordan River. Then Moses began to speak to the Israelites. All of them were either very young or were unborn at the time of the exodus from Egypt. In the first three chapters, Moses told them many of the historical things of the past forty years, including the appointment of leaders and sending out of spies into Canaan and the rebellion that followed.

Moses explained that they did not invade Canaan thirty-nine years earlier because the people did not trust God to deliver them from the enemy.

As a result, God was angry with them and swore that no one from that generation would enter the Promised Land. There were two exceptions, Caleb and Joshua. They were the two spies among the twelve who believed that God had already given them the victory.

A. Moses Discusses the Covenant Made at Mount Sinai
Deuteronomy 4:1–6:9

Then Moses warned the Israelites to listen carefully to the laws he was about to teach them. He told them that if they followed these laws, they would live and be able to enter Canaan and take the land God had promised to their ancestors.

Moses, trying to educate and encourage the people, reminded them how the Ten Commandments were first given to the people by God. Then he continued by telling them to obey God's laws and to teach them to their children so that they may teach them to their children.

> You came near and stood at the foot of the mountain
> while it blazed with fire to the very heavens, with black

clouds and deep darkness. Then the LORD spoke to you out of the fire. You heard the sound of words but saw no form; there was only a voice. He declared to you his covenant, the Ten Commandments, which he commanded you to follow and then wrote them on two stone tablets. And the LORD directed me at that time to teach you the decrees and laws you are to follow in the land that you are crossing the Jordan to possess. (Deuteronomy 4:11–14 NIV)[109]

Moses continued to talk about the covenant and the proper relationship with God.

Love the LORD your God with all your heart and with all your soul and with all your strength. These commandments that I give you today are to be on your hearts. Impress them on your children. Talk about them when you sit at home and when you walk along the road, when you lie down and when you get up. Tie them as symbols on your hands and bind them on your foreheads. Write them on the doorframes of your houses and on your gates. (Deuteronomy 6:4–9 NIV)[110]

B. The One Place of Worship
Deuteronomy 12:2–7

Moses also gave directions for worshipping God once the people got into Canaan. He instructed them to completely destroy all the worship places of the Canaanites, whether on high mountains, under trees, or anyplace else the Canaanites might be worshipping their gods. They were also told to break down the altars, smash their sacred stones, and burn down their Asherah poles. They were to cut down the idols of the Canaanites' gods. And they were absolutely forbidden from worshipping any of the Canaanites' gods.

Moses told them of the special feasts and ceremonies that must be carried out through the year. These had been explained to the previous generation in Exodus, Leviticus, and Numbers.

C. The King
Deuteronomy 17:14–20

God wanted to be the Israelites' king. God's covenant with humans did not include a king over Israel. God wanted a direct relationship with humans, but He knew that once the Israelites settled in the Promised Land, they would look at the other nations around them and want a king like they had.

Therefore, in advance, God gave the Israelites some guidelines for selecting their king.

1. Appoint a king the Lord chooses.
2. He must be an Israelite, not a foreigner.
3. He must not acquire large numbers of horses.
4. He must not make the people return to Egypt to get horses.
5. He must not take many wives, or his heart will be led astray.
6. He must not accumulate large amounts of gold and silver.
7. He must write on a scroll for himself a copy of the law.
8. He must keep the scroll with him and read it every day.
9. He must not turn away from the law.
10. He must not consider himself better than his fellow Israelites.

D. The Prophet
Deuteronomy 18:14–22

Moses warned the Israelites not to listen to the prophets of the other peoples around them. Prophets from other nations practiced sorcery and divination.

Instead, Moses told the people that God would raise up a prophet like him from among his own people. He reminded them of their request at Mount Horeb, when they heard the voice of God, saw His great fire, and were sure they were going to die. This new prophet would be sent to speak to them. They must listen to this prophet because God had promised to put His words in the mouth of this new prophet.

Any prophet who pretends to speak for God or speaks for any other gods must be put to death.

Moses told the people how to tell a prophet of God from a false prophet.

> If what a prophet proclaims in the name of the LORD does not take place or come true, that is a message the LORD has not spoken. (Deuteronomy 18:22 NIV)[111]

E. Recommitting to the First Covenant
Deuteronomy 26:16–19

Moses explained to the Israelites that they must accept the terms for the covenant relationship between God and the Israelites that was made at Mount Sinai.

> The LORD your God commands you this day to follow these decrees and laws; carefully observe them with all your heart and with all your soul. You have declared this day that the LORD is your God and that you will walk in His ways, that you will keep his decrees, commands, and law, and that you will obey Him. And the LORD has declared this day that you are His people, His treasured possession as He promised, and that you are to keep all His commands. He has declared that He will set you in praise, fame and honor high above all the nations He has made and that you will be a people holy to the LORD your God, as He promised. (Deuteronomy 26:16–19 NIV)[112]

F. Blessings for Obedience
Deuteronomy 28:1–14

Here are just some of the many blessings God promised the Israelites for obeying His law.

1. Your nation will be set high above other nations.
2. You will be blessed in all your coming and going and your work will be prosperous.
3. Your enemies who rise up against you will suffer defeat.
4. All the people of the earth will fear you because you are God's chosen people.
5. You will lend to many nations but will not need to borrow.

G. Curses for Disobedience
Deuteronomy 28:15–68

The following are some of the curses for disobedience.

1. You will be cursed and fail at everything you do.
2. You will fail wherever you go.
3. You will experience confusion and rebuke in all things.
4. You will be struck with wasting disease, fever and inflammation.
5. You will suffer heat and drought.
6. The land will fail you.
7. You will suffer defeat at the hands of your enemies.
8. Your livestock will suffer.
9. Your relationships will suffer.

H. Renewal of the Covenant between God and the Israelites
Deuteronomy 29:1–30:5

Moses recounted the circumstances and events from before the exodus to the first attempt to enter the Promised Land. Many of the people, when they were young, saw all that the Lord did in Egypt to Pharaoh, to his officials, and to his land. Yet the Israelites didn't seem to understand that these things were revealing the great power and love that God had for His chosen people.

Moses pointed out to them that during the forty years in the wilderness, their clothes did not wear out, and neither did their sandals. They ate no bread and drank no wine or other fermented drink, but they did have water. The Lord did all this so the people would know that He was their God.

The armies of two kings, Sihon and Og, came out to fight the Israelites, but Israel defeated them and took their land. The land was given as an inheritance to the tribes of Reuben and Gad, and to the half tribe of Manasseh.

Moses then warned the people to take the covenant seriously. He told them they were standing in the presence of the LORD your God for the purpose of making and sealing a covenant with God.

The terms of the covenant were as follows.

1. God (Yahweh) would be Israel's God, as He had promised them and had sworn to their fathers, Abraham, Isaac, and Jacob.
2. The parties to the covenant would also include those Israelites who were no longer able to be present (dead).
3. The Israelites must make sure that there is no one among them whose heart might turn away from the LORD their God to go and worship the gods of other nations.

Once again, because of His great love for His creation, God offered a remedy of His own making.

> When all these blessings and curses I have set before you come on you and you take them to heart wherever the LORD your God disperses you among the nations, and when you and your children return to the LORD your God and obey him with all your heart and with all your soul according to everything I command you today,

then the LORD your God will restore your fortunes and
have compassion on you and gather you again from
all the nations where he scattered you. Even if you
have been banished to the most distant land under the
heavens, from there the LORD your God will gather you
and bring you back. He will bring you to the land that
belonged to your ancestors, and you will take possession
of it. He will make you more prosperous and numerous
than your ancestors. (Deuteronomy 30:1–5 NIV)[113]

I. Transfer of Leadership
Deuteronomy 31:1–8

Moses called the people together to announce a change of leadership.
He pointed out that he was 120 years old and no longer able to lead the
people. He shared with them, again, that the Lord had said that he would
not be allowed to cross the Jordan.

He also stated that the Lord would cross the Jordan before them and
destroy the nations before the Israelites. This didn't mean that He would
destroy the nations and Israel could simply walk in and set up house. It
meant that as the Israelites went into Canaan, resistance they met would
be conquered by Israel with God's help, and Israel would take their land.

Moses, wanting to encourage them, stated again that the Lord would
deliver all these nations to the Israelites and that they had to do to them
what God had told them to do.

He then told them to be strong and courageous and not to be afraid,
because the Lord would go with them. God would never leave or forsake
them.

Then Moses performed the transfer of leadership.

Then Moses summoned Joshua and said to him in the
presence of all Israel, "Be strong and courageous, for you
must go with this people into the land that the LORD

swore to their ancestors to give them, and you must divide it among them as their inheritance. The Lord himself goes before you and will be with you; he will never leave you nor forsake you. Do not be afraid; do not be discouraged." (Deuteronomy 31:7–8 NIV)[114]

J. Public Reading of the Law
Deuteronomy 31:9–13

> So Moses wrote down this law and gave it to the Levitical priests, who carried the ark of the covenant of the Lord, and to all the elders of Israel. (Deuteronomy 31:9 NIV)[115]

Moses then directed them to read this law before the people every seven years during a ceremony called the Feast of the Tabernacles. This festival always occurred at a location chosen by God, and it included the forgiving of all debts. All Israel was required to attend. "All Israel" included men, women, children, and foreigners residing in the Israelite towns.

The intent was to create an opportunity for people to listen and learn to fear the Lord God, and to follow carefully all the words of this law. Any child who did not know this law was required to listen to it and learn to fear the Lord.

This custom was required for as long as Israel was living in the land taken from Canaan.

K. The Song of Moses
Deuteronomy 32:1–43

Moses wrote a song that reflected on the covenant between God and humans from creation to the present. It's a beautiful and sensitive psalm that deserves to be read and thought about. It can be found in Deuteronomy 32.

Moses recited the words from beginning to end in front of the whole assembly of Israel.

On that same day, God told Moses to go up Mount Nebo in Moab, across from Jericho, and view Canaan. God also told him that he would die there and be gathered to his people, like Aaron had died on Mount Hor and was gathered to his people.

The phrase "gathered to his people" is common in ancient Near East literature. It was customary to bury family members together, and people generally assumed that in the afterlife, their social relationship would continue.[116]

L. Moses Dies
Deuteronomy 34:1–7

As God said would happen, Moses went up to the top of Mount Nebo. From there, God showed him the whole land.

Then Moses died in Moab. He was buried by God in the valley opposite Beth Peor.

SECTION 5—SIN AND FORGIVENESS

In chapter 4:25–31, Moses told the people what would happen to them if they entered into the Promised Land and then forgot to worship God as they should.

> After you have had children and grandchildren and have lived in the land a long time—if you then become corrupt and make any kind of idol, doing evil in the eyes of the LORD your God and arousing his anger, I call the heavens and the earth as witnesses against you this day that you will quickly perish from the land that you are crossing the Jordan to possess. You will not live there long but will certainly be destroyed. The LORD

will scatter you among the peoples, and only a few of you will survive among the nations to which the LORD will drive you. There you will worship man-made gods of wood and stone, which cannot see or hear or eat or smell. (Deuteronomy 4:25–28 NIV)[117]

Note in the preceding verses that Moses foretells

1. the rebellion of the people against the laws of God,
2. their resulting defeats, and
3. exile among the conquering nations (about nine hundred years into the future).

In the scripture quoted earlier, the literary form "I call the heavens and the earth as witnesses against you" (Deuteronomy 4:26) is that of a contract and curse for breach of the contract. For a contract to be valid in the ancient Near East, there had to be witnesses. This procedure is followed even today.

It is important that even though there is a curse for breach of the covenant, God also provides a remedy.

But if from there you seek the LORD your God, you will find him if you seek him with all your heart and with all your soul. When you are in distress and all these things have happened to you, then in later days you will return to the LORD your God and obey him. For the LORD your God is a merciful God; he will not abandon or destroy you or forget the covenant with your ancestors, which he confirmed to them by oath. (Deuteronomy 4:29–31 NIV)[118]

The remedy is to

1. seek the Lord your God with all your heart and with all your soul, and
2. return to the Lord your God and obey Him.

This is the pattern of human behavior that you see all through the Old Testament. Take a vow, break it, suffer for breaking it, feel bad, and then call on God. If God hears a sincere prayer of confession and repentance, then God forgives.

In the Old Testament, confession and repentance involved proper ceremonial sacrifice. The sacrifice was specific to a certain sin or group of sins. The next time you committed a sin, you were condemned all over again. The condemnation was on you until the next sin sacrifice.

Also, if the sin sacrifice had not been properly presented, then it failed to meet the standard for your sin removal. Therefore, you were still condemned by your sin.

Today, we repeat the same cycle: sin, suffer guilt, call on God and repent, and hope for forgiveness. So what's the difference?

The difference is the sacrifice. God himself presented our sin sacrifice for us, so it was presented perfectly. Animal sacrifice fell short of God's requirement for humans. But God didn't sacrifice an animal for us. He sacrificed His own Son, Jesus Christ, in our place. Death was the penalty for sin. We sinned, so we should have been the ones to die.

It was God's plan, from the beginning, that God would sacrifice His own Son. It had to be His Son because only Jesus could become man and live a perfect life so that the sacrifice was perfect in every way. When Jesus died in our place, He paid for all sin—past, present, and future. Since the sacrifice and resurrection of Jesus, there has no longer been the need for the ceremonial sacrifices. The debt has been paid; we simply have to show up and accept it by faith.

Faith is the key to the successful application of the sacrifice of Christ to us, resulting in the forgiveness of all our sins. The Israelites had hoped that their sin sacrifice was good enough to wash away their sins. But our hope is in Jesus Christ as our sin sacrifice. The sacrifice was perfect. The Lamb was perfect. We must have the faith, a solid belief that the sacrifice of Jesus covered all our sins, in order for our sins to be forgiven. This is why Christianity is a faith-based religion, not a works-based religion. There's nothing that we can do to gain salvation. It's what we believe, not what we do, that gains us salvation.

In the letter to the Hebrews, the writer declares,

> Now faith is confidence in what we hope for and assurance about what we do not see. (Hebrews 11:1 NIV)[119]

In Paul's letter to the Romans, he states it clearly.

> If you declare with your mouth, "Jesus is Lord," and believe in your heart that God raised him from the dead, you will be saved. (Romans 10:9 NIV)[120]

SECTION 6—DISCUSSION QUESTIONS

1. What is a covenant?
2. Why, in Deuteronomy, did Moses repeat so much information from Genesis, Exodus, Leviticus, and Numbers?
3. What big event was Moses preparing the Israelites for when they were camped in the area of Mount Nebo?
4. Who was Moses's successor, and why was he picked for the job?
5. Who were the only two old guys allowed to enter the Promised Land? Why?
6. What were two prophecies Moses made concerning the Israelites after they entered the Promised Land?
7. Why was it necessary for there to be a public reading of the law?
8. What psalm did Moses write?
9. What items were carried in the ark?
10. Which tribal members were allowed to touch the ark?

SECTION 7—DEUTERONOMY HEADINGS

The Song of Moses	31:30–32:47
Moses to Die on Mount Nebo	32:48–32:52
Moses Blesses the Tribes	33:1–33:29
The Death of Moses	34:1–34:12

Two Things I Will Remember About the Book of Deuteronomy:

1. _____
   _____

2. _____
   _____

Think about what you have learned in the book of Deuteronomy. Pick two things that you think you can easily remember and write them above. If you need a little help, read through the headings listed in section 7, or reread sections 3–6. There are no "best" answers. List what first comes to your mind. That is the information that you are most likely to remember over a long period of time.

Refer back to this page regularly to refresh your memory.

CHAPTER 6
JOSHUA

In this chapter, you will get a grip on when, where, and how the Israelite nation entered into the Promised Land. The book of Joshua is named after the lead character in the book. He was the last individual leader of the Israelites, as a nation, until the era of the kings.

SECTION 1—REVIEW

After the Hebrew slaves left Egypt with Moses, they entered a covenant with God. Basically, the agreement was that if the Israelites would obey God, God would bless them by taking care of their needs, giving them a place to live, the Promised Land, and giving them military victories and long life.

However, the Israelites rebelled and failed to keep their part of the agreement numerous times. As a result, that generation was not allowed to go into the Promised Land. The generation after them, their children, entered a new covenant with God and were allowed to enter the Promised Land.

Moses died outside the Promised Land and was buried by God. Joshua, the assistant to Moses, replaced Moses as the leader of the nation of Israel. The structure of priests, tribal leaders, and judges remained in place but was unified under the leadership of Joshua.

SECTION 2—PREFACE

The major theme of the book of Joshua is the entry into and conquest of the Promised Land. However, the Israelites did not conquer all the areas that God had given them. Conquering included the expulsion of the Canaanites from their areas. Few of the tribes actually did that. Instead, they chose to coexist with the Canaanites—something that was explicitly forbidden unless the Canaanites converted to Yahweh.

As you read the material, you will see the familiar pattern of disobedience, oppression, repentance, and delivery. Also, you will see that, as in all scripture, God reveals more about His own nature and about His desired relationship with His people.

Remember the nature of God's covenant with humans. It is founded on God's love and faithfulness, and His patience and forgiveness. God requires the love of humans, which is expressed in obedience. Jesus, the Son of God, requires the same thing.

> If you love me, you will keep my commandments. (John 14:15 NIV)[121]

In return for that love, God pledges to provide and care for humans in all situations, if only humans will trust Him in those situations.

The dilemma posed by the sin-nature of humans is that they are rebellious and incapable of consistently pleasing God. Yet God tells us,

> I am the LORD your God; consecrate yourselves and be holy, because I am holy. (Leviticus 11:44 NIV)[122]

God prescribed ceremonial cleansing as a temporary means of making the Israelites holy. That enabled God to dwell among them. But ceremonial cleansing was only temporary. In a very short time, they became unclean again through sin.

God Himself provides in the New Testament the final fix for our sin. It isn't by obedience—humans are really lousy at being obedient. It is by faith in the one man who was obedient and fulfilled the covenant with God for all of us: Jesus Christ, our Lord and Savior!

As you read this material, you will become familiar with the following.

1. The leadership structure of the Israelites,
2. The relationship between God and the new generation of Israelites,
3. A miracle performed by God when the Israelites tried to cross the Jordan River, which was at flood stage,
4. The reason the Israelites were able to defeat the Canaanites, and
5. The Israelites' ability/inability to keep the covenant with God.

SECTION 3—GENERAL

Author:[123] No one knows for sure. The early Jews say Joshua wrote all of it except the part about his death. Today, after careful study of the book, many scholars think it was written well after Joshua's death.

Date Written:[124] About 1390 BC.

Period Covered:[125] Between 1406 BC and 1375 BC.

Audience:[126] Israelites born after the Jews had entered the Promised Land.

Cultural Setting:[127] Joshua takes up where Deuteronomy leaves off.

Historical Setting: Late Bronze Age (1550–1200 BC).[128] The major powers who had been in the area—the Hittites, the Babylonians, and the Egyptians—no longer had a significant presence. The Israelites faced many individual city-states as opposed to a large, consolidated people.[129]

SECTION 4—JOSHUA

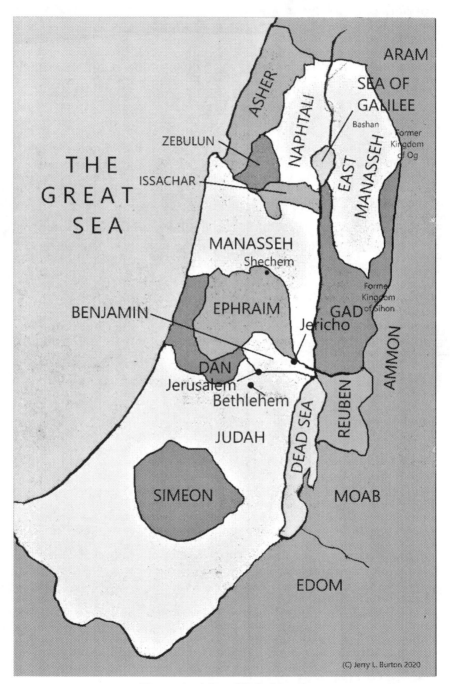

Figure 6.1. Map of Tribal Lands

In Figure 6.1, the approximate starting position of Joshua was east of Jericho and the Jordan River, on the border between Reuben and Gad. Note the areas formerly belonging to King Og and King Sihon. This is the Transjordan area, where three of the tribes settled before Israel crossed the Jordan into Canaan.

The Lord told Joshua to get ready to cross the Jordan River into the land that God is about to give to the Israelites. He had told Joshua how much land would be given to each tribe and what the boundaries would be. God also assured Joshua that no one would be able to stand against him for the rest of his life. God said that He would never leave Joshua.

God told Joshua to obey the law given to the Hebrews by Moses and that his success depended on it. He also told Joshua that he should memorize the law and think about it all the time. God promised that if Joshua did as He said, he would be prosperous and successful.

God then told Joshua to be strong and courageous. Joshua shouldn't be afraid or become discouraged. God reassured Joshua that He would be with him wherever he went.

Joshua told all the people that in three days, they would cross the Jordan River into Canaan.

Three days later, all the Israelites crossed the Jordan except the wives, children, and livestock of three tribes Reuben, Gad, and Manasseh. They remained on their land, east of the Jordan. Their land was the land that had belonged to the conquered kings, Sihon and Og. However, the soldiers from those three tribes continued across the Jordan, as they had agreed to do in Numbers 32:31–33. Reference Figure 6.1.

As the Canaanites were driven out of each piece of the Promised Land, the nation (tribe) to whom God had promised that land would stay there and maintain control over it. All the other soldiers continued to the next battle.

After they had helped the other tribes conquer their land, the soldiers from Reuben, Gad, and Manasseh returned across the Jordan to their own lands and families.

A. Rahab and the Spies
Chapter 2:1–24

As a military man, Joshua was concerned about the strength and defenses of Jericho, so he sent two spies into the city. The spies entered the city and stayed in the house of a prostitute named Rahab.

The king of Jericho received word that there were spies in Rahab's house, so he sent men there to catch them. However, Rahab had hidden them. She told the king's men that the spies had left as the sun was going down. The king's men then left to chase the spies.

After the king's men had left, the spies lay down to sleep for the night. Rahab went up on the roof and slept there. Before she went up on the roof, she told the two spies that she knew the Lord had given them this land and that everyone in the city was afraid of the Israelites. The whole city knew of all the things the Israelites had been able to do because the Lord was with them. Rahab said,

> Now then, please swear to me by the LORD that you
> will show kindness to my family, because I have shown
> kindness to you. Give me a sure sign that you will spare
> the lives of my father and mother, my brothers and
> sisters, and all who belong to them—and that you will
> save us from death. (Joshua 2:12–13 NIV)[130]

The two spies agreed but told her that she couldn't tell anyone else what they were doing. She agreed and let them down by a rope through a window. Her house was part of the city wall, so the men were outside the city wall when they got to the ground. The spies told her that she should tie a scarlet cord in the window. This would keep her safe once the attack started. The spies left, and she tied the scarlet cord in the window.

When the spies got back to their camp, they told Joshua about the help they had received from the woman, Rahab. The spies also told him that they had instructed her to tie a scarlet cord in her window and that she and her family would not be harmed when the city was attacked. Then they told Joshua,

> The LORD has surely given the whole land into our hands; all the people are melting in fear because of us. (Joshua 32:24 NIV)[131]

B. Crossing the Jordan
Chapter 3:1–5:1

When the time came, Joshua and all the Israelites set out with the ark of the covenant leading the way. The people were told to stay roughly half a mile behind the ark. No one was to touch it.

When they reached the Jordan River, the Jordan was at flood stage. The Lord had told Joshua to tell the priests who would be carrying the ark of the covenant,

> When you reach the edge of the Jordan's waters, go and stand in the river. (Joshua 3:8 NIV)[132]

Joshua then told the people how they would know that the living God was with them and would do all He had promised. They would see that the ark of the covenant was going into the Jordan before them.

The people broke camp and moved toward the Jordan. They could see the priests carrying the ark of the covenant ahead of them. When the priests with the ark stepped into the Jordan, the water from upstream stopped flowing. Sure enough, the water piled up on the upstream side, and the water flowing down to the Dead Sea was completely cut off.

The people crossed over the Jordan opposite Jericho. In the middle of the Jordan River, the priests who carried the ark of the covenant of the Lord stopped. They stood there on dry ground until the whole nation crossed over.

After all the people had crossed, one person from each tribe was told to go back into the dry riverbed. They went to the center where the priests were. There, they picked up a large stone and carried it to the other side of the Jordan, where the nation waited.

Then the priests carrying the ark of the covenant came out of the river bed. Immediately, the waters of the Jordan returned to flood stage. That night, the Israelites camped there. They were at Gilgal, on the eastern border of Jericho.

Joshua piled the stones up as a memorial to the crossing of the Jordan River. In all, about forty thousand men, all armed for battle, had crossed over.

When all the Amorite kings west of the Jordan and all the Canaanite kings along the coast heard how the Lord had dried up the Jordan so the Israelites could cross, they were filled with fear.

C. The Fall of Jericho
Chapter 5:13–6:27

As Joshua was nearing Jericho, he saw a man standing in front of him with his sword drawn. Joshua asked the man if he was a friend or an enemy.

The man told Joshua that he was appearing to him as the commander of the Lord's army. Joshua fell facedown to the ground in reverence, and asked him,

> What message does my Lord have for his servant? (Joshua 5:14 NIV)[133]

The commander of the Lord's army told Joshua to take off his sandals because he was standing on holy ground. Joshua took off his sandals. Joshua then knew that God surely was with him.

The city of Jericho had locked their gates and were not letting anyone go in or out because of the Israelites.

But the Lord told Joshua that He had delivered Jericho into his hands. Then, the Lord told Joshua His plan.

1. For six days, you are to march around the city once with all the armed men. Each day, have seven priests carry trumpets of rams' horns in front of the ark as the armed men marched around the city.
2. On the seventh day, they should march around the city seven times, with the priests blowing the trumpets.
3. Then, have the priests sound a long blast on the trumpets and have the whole army give a loud shout.

That was it. The wall of the city would collapse, and the army could go straight in.

Joshua called the priests together and told them the plan. He ordered the army to march around the city in front of the ark, but not to give the war cry or even raise their voices until the day he told them to shout.

For six days, the army marched around the city one time and then returned to camp to spend the night.

Then on the seventh day, they all got up at the crack of dawn and marched around the city just as they had done before. This time, they circled the city seven times. The seventh time around, the priests sounded the trumpets. Joshua shouted,

> Shout! For the LORD has given you the city! The city and all that is in it are to be devoted to the LORD. (Joshua 6:16–17 NIV)[134]

The Hebrew word for *devoted* as used above is *herem*. This word calls for something or someone to be made ineligible for human use.[135]

Just as the Lord had said, the wall fell down, and the Israelite army was able to go straight into the city.

Everything in the city, men and women, young and old, and cattle, sheep, and donkeys, was killed except for Rahab and all who were with her in her house. They brought out her entire family and put them in a place outside the camp of Israel.

All the silver and gold and the articles of bronze and iron were put into the treasury of the Lord's house. Then they burned the whole city and everything in it. When that had been done, Joshua put a curse on the ruins of the city of Jericho.

> Cursed before the LORD is the one who undertakes to rebuild this city, Jericho: "At the cost of his firstborn son he will lay its foundations; at the cost of his youngest he will set up its gates." (Joshua 6:26 NIV)[136]

Later in scripture, this curse actually falls on a man who decides to rebuild Jericho. Reference 1 Kings 16:34.

D. Achan's Sin
Joshua 7:1–26

Next, Joshua sent some soldiers to Ai to take that town, but they were defeated badly. Joshua realized something had gone very wrong. For God to have not given the army a victory there, someone must have done something offensive to God.

On your own, read the story of Achan and what he did that offended God. I've given you the beginning of the story. The rest of the story is recorded in Joshua 7:6–26.

E. The Sun Stands Still
Joshua 10:1–15

This story involves a battle during which Joshua received a very strange assist from God. The armies of five kings had attacked Gibeon because the king of Gibeon had made a treaty of peace with the Israelites.

The Gibeonites were terribly outnumbered and had sent a message to Joshua asking for help.

Joshua responded and was winning the battle, but because of the large number of enemy, night would fall before the battle could be completed; the enemy could slip away under the cover of darkness. Start reading at Joshua 10:6 and read through verse 15.

There is an excellent article in the NIV Cultural Backgrounds Study Bible that shifts the interpretation from one of a physical disruption of natural phenomena to one of ancient Near Eastern omens. It's well worth reading. My oversimplified summation of the article is that the reference to the sun standing still and the moon stopping for a day is really a reference to the relative position of the sun and the moon being visible in opposite parts of the sky. This happens when the sun rises before the moon sets. The emphasis is on opposite. When the moon sets and then the sun comes up, the sun and the moon are said to be in harmony. If opposition occurs at the wrong time of the month, which is when this battle is occurring, then it would be interpreted as a bad omen.

The Amorites would have placed significant meaning in this sign. It would have been enough for them to give up the battle.[137]

I hope that reading these two short stories helps you gain not only knowledge but confidence in your ability to read and understand God's Word.

F. Division of the Remainder of the Land
Chapter 18:1–19:48

The fight against the whole land of Canaan took many years. Eventually the fighting stopped, but seven of the Israelite tribes had not yet settled in their land. Those seven tribes were the following.

1. Benjamin
2. Simeon

3. Zebulun
4. Issachar
5. Asher
6. Naphtali
7. Dan

Joshua called the tribes together. He was very upset that these seven tribes had not occupied the land that God had given them. Joshua told each of these seven tribes to appoint three men. These men were then sent out to survey the land that had not been occupied and write a description of each of the pieces of land.

After they had done this, the descriptions were given to Joshua. Joshua then cast lots to see which tribes would get which lands. The division of the rest of the land was settled, but each of the seven tribes would have to go fight the Canaanites still living in those areas.

G. Eastern Tribes Return Home
Chapter 22:1–34

Joshua called together the soldiers from the three tribes whose land was on the eastern side of the Jordan. They had helped the other tribes defeat the Canaanites. Now, Joshua thanked these soldiers and let them go back to their homes and families on the eastern side of the Jordan.

H. Joshua's Farewell to the Leaders
Chapter 23:1–16

All the tribes got settled in their assigned areas and lived in peace for a long time.

When Joshua was very old and near to his death, he asked all the people and leaders of Israel to gather around him. He reminded them of everything that God had done for them. He made a speech and in it, he reminded them of the following.

1. It was God who had fought for Israel and had driven out the Canaanites.
2. Be careful to obey everything in the book of the law of Moses.
3. Do not associate with the nations around them.
4. Do not worship or swear by any of the gods of these surrounding nations.

Joshua made clear to them that their victories in battle and their strength came from God. When God fought for them, one of their soldiers was equal to a thousand of the enemy.

Finally, Joshua reminded the Israelites that if they violated the covenant of the Lord their God and served other gods and bowed down to them, the Lord's anger would burn against them, and they would quickly perish from the good land God had given them. He told them to be very careful to love the Lord their God.

I. The Covenant Renewed at Shechem
Chapter 24:1–28

Once again, Joshua felt the covenant needed to be renewed. He assembled all the tribes of Israel at Shechem and reminded them that God had made a covenant of love long ago to their forefathers, Abraham, Isaac, and Jacob. He told the stories of God moving Abraham and his family from another land to the land of Canaan, and how God had promised to give that land to him and make him the father of a great nation.

He told them of Jacob taking his family to Egypt so they would survive the famine. Then he reminded the people that God had sent Moses and Aaron to take them out of slavery in Egypt.

After wandering in the wilderness, they conquered the Amorites on the east side of the Jordan River. Then, they crossed the Jordan and conquered the nations there. God Himself drove out many of their enemies.

Joshua told them they needed to declare their loyalty to God and renew the covenant that Moses had with God. Joshua told them to fear the Lord and serve him faithfully. He challenged them to throw away the false gods of their ancestors and of those nations around them, and to serve the Lord.

Then, Joshua told them that they needed to choose whom they would serve. If serving the Lord seemed undesirable to them, then they should clearly choose to serve whatever other gods they wanted. Joshua said,

> But as for me and my household, we will serve the Lord. (Joshua 24:15 NIV)[138]

Joshua warned them that God is a holy God and a jealous God. If they were rebellious, He would not forgive their rebellion or their sins. If the people served foreign gods, God would bring disaster on them.

The people told Joshua that they would serve the Lord.

So, on that day in Shechem, the people reaffirmed the covenant with God. Then Joshua took a large stone and set it up there under the oak near the holy place of the Lord. The stone was a "witness" to the covenant made with God.

J. Buried in the Promised Land
Chapter 24:29–33

Joshua died at the age of 110. He was buried at Timnath Serah in the hill country of Ephraim, north of Mount Gaash. That was an area in the part of the Promised Land that was his inheritance.

You may remember that when the Israelites left Egypt, they brought Joseph's bones with them. They buried Joseph's bones at Shechem. Joseph was buried in the tract of land that Jacob had bought from the sons of Hamor, the father of Shechem.

Eleazar, son of Aaron, died and was also buried in the hill country of Ephraim.

SECTION 5—DISCUSSION QUESTIONS

1. What was the leadership structure of the Israelite nation after the death of Moses?
2. How many spies were sent into the city of Jericho?
3. Who was the woman in Jericho who took in the spies?
4. What color was the cord hung from the window in Jericho?
5. Who led the way across the Jordan, and what were they carrying?
6. What miracle did God perform that was similar to one He performed for Moses?
7. Where did the tribes of Reuben, Gad, and Manasseh settle?
8. Whose land was taken by the tribes of Reuben, Gad, and Manasseh, and how did they get it?
9. What was the reason the Israelites were able to defeat the Canaanites?
10. After the death of Joshua, who were the leaders of the Israelites?
11. Where was Joshua buried?
12. What did God tell the Israelites about their ability to keep the covenant with God?
13. What happened at Shechem?
14. In whom do we hope for our salvation?

SECTION 6—JOSHUA HEADINGS

Joshua Installed as Leader	1:1–1:18
Rahab and the Spies	2:1–2:24
Crossing the Jordan	3:1–5:1
Circumcision and Passover at Gilgal	5:2–5:12
The Fall of Jericho	5:13–6:27
Achan's Sin	7:1–7:26
Ai Destroyed	8:1–8:29

Two Things I Will Remember About the Book of Joshua:

1. _____

   _____

2. _____

   _____

Think about what you have learned in the book of Joshua. Pick two things that you think you can easily remember and write them above. If you need a little help, read through the headings listed in section 6, or reread sections 3–5. There are no "best" answers. List what first comes to your mind. That is the information that you are most likely to remember over a long period of time.

Refer back to this page regularly to refresh your memory.

CHAPTER 7
JUDGES

In this chapter, you will get a grip on the culture of the nation of Israel in which people did what was right in their own minds. It was a very dark time in the history of the nation.

With Joshua gone, there was no central leadership, militarily or morally. What had been a nation was nothing more than a loose confederation of tribes. That happened because the people turned away from Yahweh and began worshipping the gods and idols of the Canaanites.

But God still loved them, so when any tribe became desperate enough to call out to God, God's Spirit would fall on one of the chosen leaders, or judges, from that tribe. That leader would be empowered to act against the source of oppression.

SECTION 1—REVIEW

While the Hebrews were still camping at the foot of Mount Sinai, Jethro, Moses's father-in-law, went to visit Moses there. Jethro noticed that every day Moses sat in a chair, surrounded by Hebrews who were upset about something one of their neighbors had said or done. All day, Moses would sit and listen to their arguments and then judge between them who was right and who was wrong, who had to pay the other, and more.

Jethro told Moses that there was a better way to do what he was doing. All these people, with all their problems, would wear out Moses. Jethro told Moses,

> Select capable men from all the people—men who fear God, trustworthy men who hated dishonest gain—and appoint them as officials over thousands, hundreds, fifties and tens. Have them serve as judges for the people at all times, but have them bring every difficult case to you; the simple cases they can decide themselves. (Exodus 18:21–22 NIV)[139]

The Israelites had been organized as a nation of tribes, and each tribe had a leader. These tribal leaders were under Moses, who in turn was under God. Moses appointed judges who would report directly to him.

Each tribe already had its own military leaders. The judges were often separate individuals; they were leaders who ruled over the daily affairs of the tribe. The people of a tribe would communicate with the judges within their own tribe.

The tribal judges communicated to Moses, and Moses communicated to God. When Moses died, Joshua took his place, and the judges reported up to him. When Joshua died, no one replaced him. It would be 340 years before Israel would have one person to lead them as a nation again.

Direct communications between God and the Israelite nation had to occur between God and the judges. As you read, notice that the communications between God and the judges generally took place in the following manner.

> The Spirit of the LORD came upon him, so that ... (Judges 3:10 NIV)[140]

SECTION 2—PREFACE

As you read, you will notice the continuing pattern of behavior in the people of Israel.

1. Disobedience
2. Oppression (hardship resulting from the actions of an enemy)
3. Repentance
4. Deliverance (rescue)

Disobedience results from many sources. Among those sources apparent in the book of Judges are the following.

1. Lack of moral leadership

   In those days Israel had no king; everyone did as they saw fit. (Judges 21:25 NIV)[141]

   Priests are not even mentioned in Judges until after the last judge, Samson.
2. Human nature is to do what one wants to do.
3. The Israelites were changing their own culture to be like the culture of the Canaanites around them. In our own culture, we call this behavior peer pressure.

Oppression results from disobeying God. In the book of Leviticus, we learned that God rewards obedience but punishes rebellion. Sometimes the punishment comes directly from God, such as the plague God sent after the people had worshipped the Golden Calf (Genesis 32:35).

In the book of Judges, instead of sending a direct punishment like a plague, God took away a reward. One of the rewards for obedience was God's protection of Israel against their evil neighbors, so God lifted His hand of protection. Then Israel's neighbors began to rule over them and force them into a hard way of life: taxes (tributes); slavery; taking their food, land, and animals; and more.

Repentance, in the Bible, means "to change your mind." In order to change your mind on something, you first have to acknowledge it. Next, you have to own it, personally. Then, you have to regret it, confess it, and ask for forgiveness. You must also try to avoid doing that thing or behavior again. God always has to be at the center of that effort because even with God's help, we still make mistakes—sometimes the same mistakes we've made before.

The people of Israel eventually cried out to God in their misery and turned away from their wicked ways. Then they remembered the covenant that the nation had made with God and recommitted themselves to it.

There's a beautiful verse in 2 Chronicles that illustrates the cycle of repentance and deliverance. After the Temple had been completed in Jerusalem, Solomon dedicated it and prepared it for God to dwell in, if He chose to. God appeared to Solomon at night and told Solomon that He was pleased with the Temple and had chosen this place for Himself as a temple for sacrifices.

God knew that the nation was weak and rebellious and would sin again. He knew that when they sinned again, He would have to punish them. But He also knew that His love for them was an everlasting love, and He would forgive and restore them.

> If my people, who are called by my name, will humble themselves and pray and seek my face and turn from their wicked ways, then I will hear from heaven, and I will forgive their sin and will heal their land. (2 Chronicles 7:14 NIV)[142]

Deliverance came from God. You will learn in Judges that God heard the cries of His people, had mercy on them, and poured His Spirit out on a judge, who then led the Israelites into battle and defeated the enemy who was oppressing them. The Israelites then turned back to God, were generally faithful, and enjoyed a good relationship with God until the judge passed away.

After the judge passed away, the pattern repeated itself: disobedience, oppression, repentance, and deliverance.

SECTION 3—GENERAL

Author:[143] The author of the book of Judges is unknown. The Jewish Talmud, a collection of traditional Jewish writings, states that Samuel wrote the book of Judges. The prophets Gad and Nathan might have contributed to the effort.

Date Written:[144] Around 1000 BC.

Period of History Covered:[145] The judges began to "rule" around 1400 BC. The period of the judges lasted until about 1050 BC.

Audience:[146] Generations of Israelites after the time of the judges. The book would remind them of their ancestors' rebellion against God and of their need of His divine deliverance.

Cultural Setting:[147] Judges appears to take up where Joshua leaves off, in the Late Bronze Age (1550–1200 BC). Many artifacts and evidence of well-developed societies have been found in the area.

As mentioned in section 1, during this time, Israel was not unified under one leader. It was a very dark time for Israel as a nation. Only a few of the tribes had actually taken control of their inheritance. The other tribes coexisted with the Canaanites. The lack of political unity caused infighting between the tribes and created the opportunity for other nations to invade them. Without a spiritual leader, the tribes began to share the spiritual culture of the Canaanites, worshipping and honoring the deities.[148]

Historical Setting:

Here are the judges discussed in the book of Judges.[149]

1.	Othniel	(3:7–11)	
2.	Ehud	(3:12–30)	c. 1309 to 1229 BC
3.	Shamgar	(3:31)	
4.	Deborah and Barak	(4–5)	c. 1209 to 1169 BC
5.	Gideon	(6–8)	c. 1162 to 1122 BC
6.	Abimelech	(9)	
7.	Tola	(10:1–2)	
8.	Jair	(10:3–5)	
9.	Jephthah	(10:6–12:7)	
10.	Ibzan	(12:8–10)	
11.	Elon	(12:11–12)	
12.	Abdon	(12:13–15)	
13.	Samson	(13–16)	c. 1075 to 1055 BC

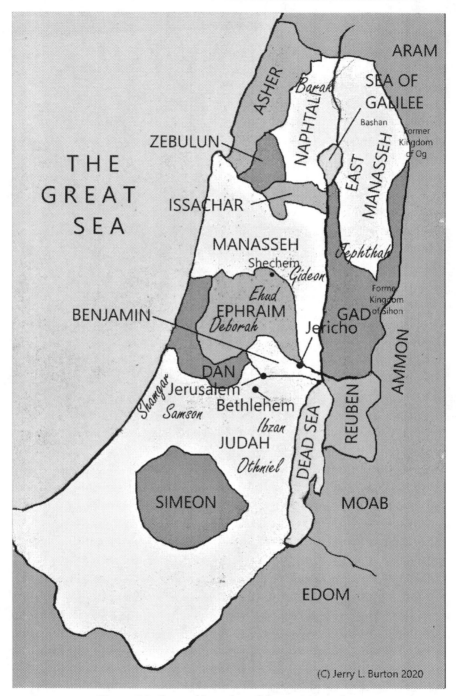

Figure 7.1. General location of the various judges

Note that Samuel, a judge, prophet, and priest, was born around 1105 BC.[150]

Only two of these judges, Deborah and Gideon, will be discussed in this workbook. However, most of them are interesting, and some are very entertaining (Ehud, for example). The story of Samson is one of the most familiar ones, and because his story is familiar, it might be a good one to read on your own. I encourage you to try.

SECTION 4—THE BOOK OF JUDGES

The book of Judges discusses, in stories, many wonderful events that demonstrate God's faithfulness to His covenant and His love for His people.

God helped the Israelites conquer many areas of the Promised Land in which the Canaanites still lived. However, in some of the areas, the Israelites did not drive all the Canaanites out of the land. Instead, the Israelites occupied the land and lived alongside the Canaanites. Before long, the cultures of the two nations became mixed. The Israelites began worshiping the false gods of the Canaanites.

God became very angry with the Israelites for turning from Him and not keeping the covenant their forefathers had made with God. Therefore, God removed his protection from them. The Canaanites began to run things and treated the Israelites very badly. Without God's help, the Israelites could not defend themselves. Whenever they would go out to fight their enemies, they would lose the battles.

The Israelites became very upset and frightened, so they cried out to God for help. God, in His love and mercy, decided to help them again. God appointed leaders called judges.

Some, but not all, of these judges were military leaders. Nor were they like the judges that Moses had appointed who helped settle disagreements and arguments between individuals, with the exception of Deborah.

The Lord selected one judge at a time, as needed, to lead the Israelites against their enemies. God was with each judge He appointed. Through the judge, God saved the people from their enemies, and there was peace for as long as the judge lived. But when the judge died, the people returned to their evil ways.

We will discuss two of these judges. Neither judge was a great military leader, but the two demonstrated a deep faith in God and submission to God's Spirit.

Deborah: Judges 4–5

Deborah was highly respected as a leader of the tribe of Ephraim. In the hill country of Ephraim between Ramah and Bethel, there was a palm tree known as the Palm of Deborah. Deborah, a judge like the ones appointed by Moses, would hold court at that tree. She would hear complaints, arguments, and questions from Israelites and make judgments about who was right and who was wrong.

But Deborah did more than this. She was also a prophet. A prophet was a person who communicated directly with God. People came to Deborah to seek God's will in their daily lives. They told Deborah what they were about to do, and Deborah would find out whether that was okay with God. Deborah would ask God about it. God then spoke to Deborah, and she would tell the person what God had said.

This service of seeking answers from God was very common during those days. There were false prophets and true prophets. Deborah was a true prophet. She sought answers only from God.

The Israelites had been under the rule of Jabin, the king of Canaan, for over twenty years. He treated them very badly, and the people of Israel cried out to God for help. God heard their cries, and because of His love for His people, He decided to help them.

God told Deborah to talk with one of Israel's military leaders and engage the Canaanite king in battle. Deborah sent for Barak, a military leader in the tribe of Naphtali. He immediately went to Deborah to see what she wanted. Deborah explained to Barak that God wanted Israel to fight with the king of Canaan and that God would help Israel win.

Barak was not happy to hear this. The commander of Canaan's army, Sisera, had "nine hundred iron chariots" at his command. Iron chariots were hard to destroy, and Israel had mainly foot soldiers and few, if any, chariots. Every nation in the Middle East feared the Canaanites and considered them impossible to defeat in battle.

The Israelites had only two things in their favor.

1. God said He would help them win
2. God had given Deborah a battle plan.

God's plan was this: Barak would gather as many soldiers as he could from his own tribe of Naphtali. Then he would get others from the tribe of Zebulun. He would take all those men up to Mount Tabor. When Sisera took his troops toward Mount Tabor, God would give the battle to Barak, and Barak would win.

Deborah told Barak of the plan. Barak said he would go if she would also go, but if she wouldn't go, then he wouldn't go either.

Deborah told Barak that of course she would go with him. However, because Barak was not willing to go without her, there would be no honor for him in winning the battle. In fact, God would deliver Sisera, the feared Canaanite military commander, into the hands of a woman, not Barak.

Barak gathered his soldiers, and with Deborah, they all went up to Mount Tabor.

When Sisera heard that Barak had taken an army up to Mount Tabor, he gathered his own army and his chariots and went toward

Mount Tabor to do battle with Barak. When Sisera got to the Kishon River, close to Mount Tabor, Barak and Deborah could see Sisera's army and chariots at the river. The chariots were of little use in mountainous terrain, so they were waiting on the flat ground by the river.

Then Deborah yelled at Barak to go; she assured him that God had gone before him and he would surely be victorious.

Barak and his men ran yelling toward Sisera's army. This caused great confusion among Sisera's army. Barak's army, running ahead of him, killed every Canaanite soldier except Sisera. During the battle, Sisera jumped from his chariot and ran away on foot.

Sisera was able to get away from the battle scene. He was looking for a place to hide when he came to a tent. The tent belonged to a woman named Jael. She went out of the tent and invited him in. She told him not to be afraid, and then she covered him with a blanket to hide him.

Sisera was thirsty and asked for a drink of water. Jael opened a skin of milk, gave him a drink, and covered him up. He asked her to stand in the doorway of the tent, and if anyone came looking for him, she should tell them that there was no one in the tent.

After a short time, Sisera fell asleep from exhaustion. Jael picked up a tent peg and a hammer. She walked quietly over to where Sisera lay fast asleep. She drove the tent peg through his temple and into the ground, and he died.

When Barak came by looking for Sisera, Jael went out to meet him. She invited Barak into the tent and showed him Sisera. There he lay, the tent peg through his temple.

As Deborah had prophesied, Sisera was killed by a woman.

The Song of Deborah was composed and sung so that Israel would remember what Deborah, Barak, Jael, and Israel had done. The song is recorded in Judges 5.

Following this, there was peace for forty years.

The manner in which God used Deborah is a great example of what the Apostle Paul said in Galatians.

> There is neither Jew nor Gentile, neither slave nor free, nor is there male and female, for you are all one in Christ Jesus. (Galatians 3:28 NIV)[151]

God uses us for His purpose based on who He is, not on who we are.

Gideon: Judges 6–8

The story of Gideon is a favorite of almost all who read it.

As is always true of the stories in the book of Judges, the Israelites had done evil in the eyes of the Lord. For seven years, God allowed the Midianites to rule over them. The Midianites were so bad to them that the Israelites built hideouts for themselves in mountain clefts and caves.

Whenever the Israelites planted their crops, the Midianites and other eastern peoples invaded their country. These foreign people camped on the land and ruined the crops. They also killed the sheep, cattle, and donkeys that belonged to the Israelites. Finally, the Israelites cried out to the Lord for help.

The Lord sent them a prophet, who reminded them of who God was and what God had done for them in the past. He also reminded them of the covenant that God had made with them and that they were to have no other gods before Him. However, they had left God and started worshipping the gods of the Amorites.

One day, Gideon was threshing wheat. Threshing is the process of beating the wheat against the floor to separate the wheat grains from the chaff (a thin shell around the grains). Usually, the threshing occurred on a threshing floor. The threshing floor was a large area of rocks, like a large patio. When the threshing floor was not being used for threshing grain, the area would become a site for public meetings.

However, Gideon wasn't threshing on a threshing floor. It was too public, and the Midianites would be able to see him and possibly attack him and take the grain for themselves. Gideon did his threshing in one of the vats, or large tubs, of a winepress.

A winepress was constructed of at least two large vats, one on top of the other. Grapes were thrown into the upper vat. Workers would then stomp around on the grapes, thus squeezing the juice out of them. The juice would run down a channel connecting the upper vat to the lower vat. The skin of the grapes would remain in the upper vat. They would be squeezed again using wooden planks. The sides of the vats were high enough that a man could easily stand and not be seen.

Basically, Gideon was hiding from the Midianites as he threshed the grain.

While Gideon was threshing, the angel of the Lord appeared to him and spoke to him, referring to him as a "mighty warrior."

Gideon then questioned what the angel of the Lord had said. Gideon felt that the Lord was not with Israel and that the Lord had abandoned them and allowed the Midianites to persecute them.

The Lord then told Gideon that he was supposed to use the strength he had and save Israel from the Midianites. The Lord reminded Gideon that He was the one sending him.

Gideon then tried to weasel out of what the Lord had told him to do. Gideon pointed out that he was from the weakest clan in his tribe, Manasseh, and that he was the least in his family.

This conversation is very much like the one between God and Moses when God had told Moses to return to Egypt and free his people. Moses kept coming up with every excuse why he could not go.

Gideon was doing the same thing.

The Lord then told Gideon that He would be with him and he would strike down all the Midianites, leaving none alive.

That seemed like a pretty big task, so Gideon wanted the Lord to give him a sign. Gideon wanted to make sure it was the Lord who had been speaking with him.

The angel of the Lord told Gideon to bring Him an offering. Gideon did and he set in on a rock. The Lord touched the offering with the tip of His staff, and the offering was consumed in fire. Then, the angel of the Lord disappeared.

Finally, Gideon realized that this had been the Lord speaking to him.

The angel reappeared to Gideon and told Gideon to tear down his father's altars to the false gods, build a proper altar to the Lord, and make a sacrifice to God on the altar. He also told Gideon to use the wood from the false altars to burn the sacrifice to God.

Gideon did as he had been told. But instead of doing it alone, he used ten of his servants to help him, and they did all of it at night instead of during the day.

The next morning, the people of the town were angry at Gideon and wanted to kill him. Gideon's father came out, faced the crowd, and talked them out of killing Gideon.

Now, all the Midianites, Amalekites, and other peoples from east of the Jordan invaded to loot Israel. It is estimated that there were 135,000 invaders.[152]

Then the Spirit of the Lord came on Gideon, and he blew a trumpet, which called the people together. He sent messengers to the other tribes, asking for soldiers.

Because Gideon lacked confidence that God would really help him, he asked God for another sign. Gideon said to God,

> I will place a wool fleece on the threshing floor. If there is dew only on the fleece and all the ground is dry, then I will know that you will save Israel by my hand, as you said. (Judges 6:37 NIV)[153]

Gideon put the fleece on the threshing floor. The next morning, the fleece was wet with dew, but the surrounding ground was dry.

Gideon, still not confident that God was going to help him, then said to God,

> Do not be angry with me. Let me make just one more request. Allow me one more test with the fleece, but this time make the fleece dry and let the ground be covered with dew. (Judges 6:39 NIV)[154]

The next morning, the fleece was dry, and all the ground was covered with dew.

Then Gideon, with about thirty-two thousand men, marched out to meet the Midianites. That night, the two armies camped a short distance from each other.

The Lord spoke to Gideon and told him that he had too many men. When the Israelites won the battle, they would forget about God helping them, and they would claim that they had won the battle by themselves.

Gideon told his army that anyone who was afraid could go home. Twenty-two thousand men left. Gideon was left with only ten thousand men.

The Lord then told Gideon that he still had too many men and to take his men down to the water and have them drink.

Gideon took the men down to the water. The Lord told him to watch how the men drank. The men who cupped the water in their hands and drank should be kept. The other men, the ones who got down on their knees and drank, had to be sent home.

Only three hundred men were left. The Lord told Gideon that with these three hundred men, He would defeat the Midianites.

The Midianites' camp was in the valley, just below Gideon's camp. During the night, the Lord told Gideon to get up and attack the Midianite camp.

> If you are afraid to attack, go down to the camp with your servant Purah and listen to what they are saying. Afterward, you will be encouraged to attack the camp. (Judges 7:10–11 NIV)

Gideon and his servant went quietly down to the edge of the camp. There, they heard a man who was telling a friend about a dream. The man said,

> I had a dream that a round loaf of barley bread came tumbling into the Midianite camp. It struck the tent with such force that the tent overturned and collapsed. (Judges 7:13–14 NIV)[155]

His friend said he thought that God had given the Midianites and the whole camp into Gideon's hands.

When Gideon heard the dream and its interpretation, he bowed down and worshiped God. He returned to the camp of Israel and called out,

> Get up! The LORD has given the Midianite camp into your hands. (Judges 7:15 NIV)[156]

Gideon divided the men into three groups and placed trumpets and empty jars in the hands of all of them. The jars had torches inside. Then, he told them to watch him.

> Follow my lead. When I get to the edge of the camp, do exactly as I do. (Judges 7:17 NIV)[157]

Gideon and the hundred men with him reached the edge of the camp at the beginning of the middle watch. The guard had just been changed. Gideon and his men blew their trumpets and broke the jars that were in their hands.

The three companies blew their trumpets and smashed the jars. Grasping the torches in their left hand and holding the trumpet in their right hand, they shouted,

> A sword for the LORD and for Gideon! (Judges 7:20 NIV)[158]

Each of Gideon's men held his position around the camp. All the Midianites ran around thinking they were under attack by a very large army! A small army would have had one to three trumpeters. The sound of three hundred trumpeters would indicate an incredibly large army.[159]

When the three hundred trumpets sounded, the Lord caused all the men in the camp to turn on each other with their swords. Many were killed in the camp. Others ran back toward their home country. The Israelites chased after the Midianites.

The escape route of the Midianites was blocked, and the Israelites were able to kill many more of the Midianites. They even captured and killed two of the Midianite leaders.

After the fighting ended, the Israelites asked Gideon to become their ruler. Gideon told them that he would not rule over them, and neither would his son. Then he said,

> The LORD will rule over you. (Judges 8:22 NIV)[160]

During Gideon's lifetime, the land had peace for forty years.

Gideon, as a man, was weak and afraid. But God was his strength and courage. God does the same for us—He is our strength and courage.

As King David later wrote,

> The LORD is my strength and my shield;
> my heart trusts in him, and he helps me.
> My heart leaps for joy,
> and with my song I praise him. (Psalm 28:7 NIV)[161]

SECTION 5—AN ASSIGNMENT, IF YOU CHOOSE TO ACCEPT IT

Please try to read the story of Samson in chapters 13–16. Then tell it to someone you know and see how you do.

SECTION 6—JUDGES HEADINGS

Israel Fights the Remaining Canaanites	1:1–1:36
The Angel of the Lord at Bokim	2:1–2:5
Disobedience and Defeat	2:6–3:6
Othniel	3:7–3:11
Ehud	3:12–3:30
Shamgar	3:31
Deborah	4:1–4:24
The Song of Deborah	5:1–5:31
Gideon	6:1–6:40
Gideon Defeats the Midianites	7:1–7:25
Zebah and Zalmunna	8:1–8:21
Gideon's Ephod	8:22–8:27
Gideon's Death	8:28–8:35

Abimelek	9:1–9:57
Tola	10:1–10:2
Jair	10:3–10:5
Jephthah	10:6–11:40
Jephthah and Ephraim	12:1–12:7
Ibzan, Elon, and Abdon	12:8–12:15
The Birth of Samson	13:1–13:25
Samson's Marriage	14:1–14:20
Samson's Vengeance on the Philistines	15:1–15:20
Samson and Delilah	16:1–16:22
The Death of Samson	16:23–16:31
Micah's Idols	17:1–17:13
The Danites Settle in Laish	18:1–18:31
A Levite and His Concubine	19:1–19:30
The Israelites Punish the Benjamites	20:1–20:48
Wives for the Benjamites	21:1–21:25

Two Things I Will Remember About the Book of Judges:

1. _____
   _____
2. _____
   _____

Think about what you have learned in the book of Judges. Pick two things that you think you can easily remember and write them above. If you need a little help, read through the "Headings" listed in section 6, above, or reread sections 3–5. There are no "best" answers. List what first comes to your mind. That is the information that you are most likely to remember over a long period of time.

Refer back to this page regularly to refresh your memory.

CHAPTER 8
RUTH

In this chapter, you will get a grip on the relationship between God and His people as reflected in the beautiful story of an Israelite widow and one of her two widowed Moabite daughters-in-law. The total devotion of the one daughter-in-law to her mother-in-law reflects the total devotion and faithfulness that we should have toward God and our neighbor.

SECTION 1—REVIEW

This story is set during the period of the judges. The nation of Israel was struggling in its relationship with God. Devotion and faithfulness were not areas of success for Israel.

SECTION 2—PREFACE

The relationship between Naomi and her daughter-in-law Ruth stands in sharp contrast to the broken relationship between Israel and her God during this period when "everyone did as they saw fit" (Judges 21:25 NIV).

SECTION 3—GENERAL

Author:[162] The author of the book of Ruth is unknown.

Date Written:[163] Around 1000 BC.

Period Covered:[164] Between 1375 BC and 1075 BC.

Audience:[165] Generations of Israelites after the time of the judges.

Cultural Setting:[166] This book offers accounts of some of the daily problems and struggles experienced by the Israelites. Many of these problems originated from the cultural environment. Many of the Israelites had chosen to coexist with the Canaanites, a people whose religious beliefs and behaviors were radically different from that demanded by Yahweh. At the same time, it illustrates the compassion and faithfulness of a foreigner, Ruth, toward her widowed mother-in-law, Naomi. Ruth reflects the faithfulness of God toward His people as well as the devotion we should have toward God, our heavenly Father. In addition, although she gives up everything to care for Naomi, she gains more than she gave up because of the graciousness of Boaz. This shadows, to some degree, the "Blessings for Obedience" found in Deuteronomy 28:1–14.

Historical Setting:[167] The book of Ruth is a personal story of one Israelite family. The events in this story occurred during the early part of the Period of the Prophets. During a famine, this family went to Moab. Their story begins about eight years before Ehud, a judge, was called by God to save Israel, and it continues for an unspecified period of time after Ehud frees Israel.

Main Themes:[168]

1. Acceptance into the family of God is based on faith and obedience.
2. Ruth's actions reflect God's own faithfulness and kindness.
3. Boaz's actions are symbolic of Christ redeeming His bride.

SECTION 4—THE BOOK OF RUTH

There was a famine in the land of Judah, location 1 in Figure 8.1. A man, Elimelek; his wife, Naomi; and their two sons, Mahlon and Kilion, went to live for a while in the country of Moab, location 2 in Figure 8.1.

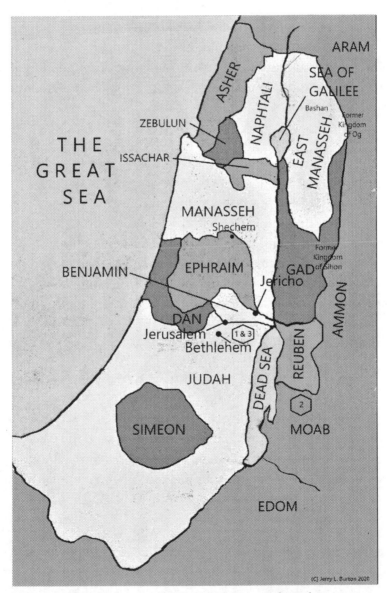

Figure 8.1. Jerusalem, Bethlehem, and Moab

While they were in Moab, Naomi's husband, Elimelek, died. After that, her two sons married Moabite women. One married a woman named Orpah, and the other married a woman named Ruth. About ten years later, the two sons died. Naomi was devastated.

When Naomi heard that God had delivered Israel from the famine, and now there was food in Israel, Naomi and her two daughters-in-law prepared to return to Israel, location 1 in Figure 8.1.

After they had set out to return to Judah, Naomi told Orpah and Ruth to return to their mothers' homes. Then she blessed the two women.

> May the LORD show you kindness, as you have shown kindness to your dead husbands and to me. May the LORD grant that each of you will find rest in the home of another husband. (Ruth 1:8–9 NIV)[169]

Naomi kissed them goodbye, and they wept. Both daughters-in-law told Naomi that they would go to Israel with her. Naomi tried to convince Orpah and Ruth to return to their own homes. Orpah kissed Naomi goodbye and walked away, but Ruth continued to cling to Naomi.

Naomi told Ruth to go back with Orpah.

Ruth's reply to Naomi is a beautiful declaration of faithfulness.

> Where you go I will go, and where you stay I will stay. Your people will be my people and your God my God. Where you die I will die, and there I will be buried. May the LORD deal with me, be it ever so severely, if even death separates you and me. (Ruth 1:16–17 NIV)[170]

Naomi finally agreed to stop urging Ruth to leave. Together, they traveled to Bethlehem. Naomi and Ruth arrived in Bethlehem at the time of the barley harvest.

Let's look back for a moment at an Israelite law concerning the harvesting of crops.

In Leviticus, God's law states,

> When you reap the harvest of your land, do not reap to the very edges of your field or gather the gleanings of your harvest. Leave them for the poor and for the foreigner residing among you. I am the LORD your God. (Leviticus 19:9–10 NIV)[171]

In Deuteronomy 24:19–22, Moses repeats this message for the new generation who will soon go into the Promised Land.

> When you are harvesting in your field and you overlook a sheaf, do not go back to get it. Leave it for the foreigner, the fatherless and the widow, so that the LORD your God may bless you in all the work of your hands. When you beat the olives from your trees, do not go over the branches a second time. Leave what remains for the foreigner, the fatherless and the widow. When you harvest the grapes in your vineyard, do not go over the vines again. Leave what remains for the foreigner, the fatherless and the widow. Remember that you were slaves in Egypt. That is why I command you to do this. (Deuteronomy 24:19–22 NIV)[172]

Both Ruth and Naomi were widows, so this law was meant to help them and others who might not have a source of income. Ruth asked permission from Naomi to go to the fields and pick up the leftover grain. Naomi said she could go.

Ruth went to a field and began to glean behind the paid workers of the field. She did not know it, but she was in the field of a man named Boaz. Boaz was actually a relative of Naomi's on her husband's side.

As Ruth was gleaning, Boaz arrived and greeted his workers. As he gazed out over the field, he saw Ruth. He asked his overseer (foreman) who this woman was.

The overseer told him that she was Ruth, the Moabite woman who had come back from Moab with Naomi. She had come into the field that morning and worked until now with only a short break.

Boaz then went to Ruth and told her not to go to any other field to work but to stay with the women who worked for him. He told her that anytime she was thirsty, she could drink.

Ruth asked Boaz why he was being so nice to her.

Boaz replied he had heard that Ruth had stayed with Naomi even though her own husband had died. He had even been told about Ruth leaving her own father and mother and her homeland to stay with Naomi and care for her.

Boaz blessed her.

> May the LORD repay you for what you have done. May you be richly rewarded by the LORD, the God of Israel, under whose wings you have come to take refuge. (Ruth 2:12 NIV)[173]

Ruth responded,

> May I continue to find favor in your eyes, my lord. You have put me at ease by speaking kindly to your servant—though I do not have the standing of one of your servants. (Ruth 2:13 NIV)[174]

At mealtime, Boaz invited her over to eat with him. He also told his men to let her gather among the sheaves (the main harvest) and once in a while to throw down some bundles they'd gathered and let her pick them up.

Ruth stayed and worked in the field until evening. Then she took what she had gathered to the threshing floor. When she was through, she took what she had gathered to her mother-in-law.

Naomi asked Ruth whose field she had worked in that day. Ruth told her that the man who owned the field was Boaz. Naomi was very pleased and told Ruth that Boaz was a close relative, very kind and one of their guardian-redeemers.

At this point, we need to look back at Leviticus to see what the law said about a guardian-redeemer.

> If one of your fellow Israelites becomes poor and sells some of their property, their nearest relative is to come and redeem what they have sold. (Leviticus 25:25 NIV)[175]

Naomi told Ruth to work with the women of Boaz's workforce. If she were to go into another field, someone might hurt her. Ruth worked in Boaz's field until the end of the harvests.

One day, Naomi told Ruth that she wanted to find a good home for her where she would be well taken care of. Then she told Ruth that Boaz would be at the threshing floor that night, and she should go down to threshing floor.

Naomi told her to wear her best clothes and put on perfume so she could make a good impression. She also told Ruth to not let Boaz know that she was there. She should wait until he had finished eating and drinking and lay down to sleep. She should watch and see where he lay down. When it was too dark for people to recognize her and Boaz was asleep, she should go over to where he was lying, uncover his feet, and lie down at his feet. After that, she should simply wait and do as he said.

Ruth did all these things.

In that culture, uncovering a man's feet and lying down was a customary, nonverbal request for marriage.[176]

In the middle of the night, Boaz woke up. There was a woman lying at his feet! In the darkness, Boaz could not tell who the woman was, so he asked, "Who are you?"

Ruth told him that she was his servant, Ruth. Then she asked Boaz to

> Spread the corner of your garment over me, since you are a guardian-redeemer of our family. (Ruth 3:9 NIV)[177]

One of the interpretations of this act is that it suggests a desire for marriage.[178]

Boaz thanked Ruth for her kindness and respect for him. He told her that the whole town thought very highly of her. Boaz also told her that he would redeem her (take care of her) except for one thing. There was another guardian-redeemer who was more closely related to Naomi than he was. This meant that the other man would have to be asked first. If the other guardian-redeemer chose to take care of Ruth and Naomi, then that was the way it would be. If not, then Boaz said he would take care of them.

Early the next morning, Ruth got up and returned home to Naomi. She shared with Naomi everything that had happened.

When Boaz got up, he went back to town and sat down at the town gate. Shortly after he sat down, the other guardian-redeemer came up to him and sat down. Then Boaz got ten of the elders to join him, and they sat down together. Boaz said to the other guardian-redeemer,

> Naomi, who has come back from Moab, is selling the piece of land that belonged to our relative Elimelek. I thought I should bring the matter to your attention and suggest that you buy it in the presence of these seated here and in the presence of the elders of my people. If you will redeem it, do so. But if you will not, tell me, so I will know. For no one has the right to do it except you, and I am next in line. (Ruth 4:3–4 NIV)[179]

The other guardian-redeemer said that he would redeem it. But then Boaz told him that when he paid Naomi for the land, he would also be getting Ruth, the Moabite who was the widow of one of Naomi's sons. He would have to take Ruth as a wife and have a son with her. This had to be done in order to maintain the name of Naomi's dead son (who was Ruth's dead husband).

The other guardian-redeemer told Boaz to buy it himself. Then he took off his sandal, indicating that the redemption and transfer of the property was final.

The other guardian-redeemer was concerned that he might lose his own estate to Ruth's children, when she had any. That was why he backed out of the redemption.

Then Boaz announced to the elders and all the people there that they were witnesses to what he had done.

1. He had bought from Naomi all the property of Elimelek, Kilion, and Mahlon.
2. He had acquired Ruth the Moabite, Mahlon's widow, as his wife in order to maintain the name of the dead with his property, and so that his name would not disappear from among his family or from his hometown.

The elders and all the people at the gate agreed that they were witnesses.

Boaz took Ruth, and she became his wife. Later, she became pregnant and gave birth to a son.

> The women said to Naomi: "Praise be to the LORD, who this day has not left you without a guardian-redeemer. May he become famous throughout Israel! He will renew your life and sustain you in your old age. For your daughter-in-law, who loves you and who is better to you than seven sons, has given him birth."

Then Naomi took the child in her arms and cared for him. The women living there said, "Naomi has a son!" And they named him Obed. He was the father of Jesse, the father of David. (Ruth 4:14–17 NIV)[180]

This David was the same David who would later kill Goliath and become the second king of Israel—and a man after God's own heart!

SECTION 5—DISCUSSION QUESTIONS

1. How would you characterize the relationship between Ruth and Naomi?
2. How would you characterize the relationship between Orpah and Naomi?
3. Which of these two women do you think characterize the desired relationship between humankind and God?
4. What characteristic or characteristics of God did Ruth demonstrate?

As Ruth sacrificed herself for Naomi, God sacrificed His son for us. Naomi could not have recovered and lived a happy life without the sacrifice that Ruth made for her. And we can't recover from sin and live an eternal life without God's sacrifice for us!

SECTION 6—RUTH HEADINGS

Naomi Loses Her Husband and Sons	1:1–1:5
Naomi and Ruth Return to Bethlehem	1:6–1:22
Ruth Meets Boaz in the Grain Field	2:1–2:23
Ruth and Boaz at the Threshing Floor	3:1–3:18
Boaz Marries Ruth	4:1–4:12
Naomi Gains a Son	4:13–4:17
The Genealogy of David	4:18–4:22

Two Things I Will Remember About the Book of Ruth:

1. _____
   _____

2. _____
   _____

Think about what you have learned in the book of Ruth. Pick two things that you think you can easily remember and write them above. If you need a little help, read through the headings listed in section 6, or reread sections 3–5. There are no "best" answers. List what first comes to your mind. That is the information that you are most likely to remember over a long period of time.

Refer back to this page regularly to refresh your memory.

ENDNOTES

1   "Author, Place and Date of Writing," in *NIV Archaeological Study Bible* (Zondervan Corporation, 2005): 2.

2   "Timeline," in *NIV Archaeological Study Bible*, 84.

3   "Author, Place and Date of Writing," in *NIV Archaeological Study Bible*, 2.

4   "Timeline," in *NIV Archaeological Study Bible*, 84.

5   *Halley's Bible Handbook* (Zondervan Corporation, 1965), 58.

6   "Timeline," in *NIV Archaeological Study Bible*, 2.

7   "Audience," in *NIV Archaeological Study Bible*, 2.

8   Magnus Mangusson, *Archaeology of the Bible* (1977): 28–29.

9   "The Historical Setting of Genesis," in *NIV Cultural Backgrounds Study Bible* (Zondervan, 2016), 26–28.

10 "Timeline," in *NIV Archaeological Study Bible*, 2.

11 *NIV Cultural Backgrounds Study Bible*, 2193.

12 *NIV Cultural Backgrounds Study Bible*, 11.

13 *NIV Cultural Backgrounds Study Bible*, 21–22.

14 "Ziggurats," in *NIV Cultural Backgrounds Study Bible*, 30.

15 *NIV Cultural Backgrounds Study Bible*, 29.

16 *NIV Cultural Backgrounds Study Bible*, 29.

17 *NIV Cultural Backgrounds Study Bible*, 29.

18 *NIV Cultural Backgrounds Study Bible*, 29–30.

19 *NIV Cultural Backgrounds Study Bible*, 33.

20 *NIV Cultural Backgrounds Study Bible*, 42–43.

21 *NIV Cultural Backgrounds Study Bible*, 43.

22 "Ratifying the Covenant," in *NIV Archaeological Study Bible*, 42–43.

23 *NIV Cultural Backgrounds Study Bible*, 44.

24 *NIV Cultural Backgrounds Study Bible*, 45.

25 *NIV Cultural Backgrounds Study Bible*, 54.

26 *NIV Cultural Backgrounds Study Bible*, 54.

27 *NIV Cultural Backgrounds Study Bible*, 55.

28 *NIV Cultural Backgrounds Study Bible*, 61.

29 *NIV Cultural Backgrounds Study Bible*, 65.

30 *NIV Cultural Backgrounds Study Bible*, 65.

31 *NIV Cultural Backgrounds Study Bible*, 89.
32 *NIV Cultural Backgrounds Study Bible*, 90.
33 *NIV Cultural Backgrounds Study Bible*, 103.
34 *NIV Cultural Backgrounds Study Bible*, 11.
35 *NIV Cultural Backgrounds Study Bible*, 11.
36 "Author, Place and Date of Writing," in *NIV Archaeological Study Bible*, 84.
37 "Timeline," in *NIV Archaeological Study Bible*, 84.
38 "Timeline," in *NIV Archaeological Study Bible*, 84.
39 "Audience," in *NIV Archaeological Study Bible*, 84.
40 "The Religion of Egypt," in *Halley's Bible Handbook*, 110–111.
41 "The Historicity of the Exodus," in *NIV Cultural Backgrounds Study Bible*, 116.
42 "Themes," in *NIV Archaeological Study Bible*, 85.
43 *NIV Cultural Backgrounds Study Bible*, 115.
44 *Halley's Bible Handbook*, 121.
45 *Halley's Bible Handbook*, 122.
46 *Halley's Bible Handbook*, 122.
47 *Halley's Bible Handbook*, 123.
48 *NIV Cultural Backgrounds Study Bible*, 128.
49 *NIV Cultural Backgrounds Study Bible*, 131.
50 *NIV Cultural Backgrounds Study Bible*, 146-148.
51 *NIV Cultural Backgrounds Study Bible*, 166.
52 *NIV Cultural Backgrounds Study Bible*, 170.
53 "Tent of meeting," in *NIV Cultural Backgrounds Study Bible*, Page 169.
54 Shaiya Rothberg, "The Politics of God's Indwelling: Jewish Public Discourse as Holy Space, The Times of Israel," October 26, 2019, https://blogs.timesofisrael.com/jewish-public-discourse-as-holy-space.
55 *NIV Cultural Backgrounds Study Bible*, 170.
56 "Author, Place and Date of Writing," in *NIV Archaeological Study Bible*, 155.
57 "Timeline," in *NIV Archaeological Study Bible*, 155.
58 "Timeline," in *NIV Archaeological Study Bible*, Page 155.
59 "Audience," in *NIV Archaeological Study Bible*, 155.
60 *Halley's Bible Handbook*, 134.
61 *Halley's Bible Handbook*, 134.
62 "Cultural Facts and Highlights," in *NIV Archaeological Study Bible*, 155.
63 Victor H. Matthews, *The Cultural World of the Bible* (2015): 48–49.
64 "Old Testament Sacrifices," in *NIV Cultural Backgrounds Study Bible*, 188.
65 *NIV Cultural Backgrounds Study Bible*, 195.
66 *NIV Cultural Backgrounds Study Bible*, 212.
67 "Key Concepts," in *NIV Cultural Backgrounds Study Bible*, 180.
68 *NIV Cultural Backgrounds Study Bible*, 209.
69 "Key Concepts," in *NIV Cultural Backgrounds Study Bible*, 180.

70 *NIV Cultural Backgrounds Study Bible*, 138.

71 *NIV Cultural Backgrounds Study Bible*, 146.

72 *NIV Cultural Backgrounds Study Bible*, 1842.

73 *NIV Cultural Backgrounds Study Bible*, 1187.

74 *NIV Cultural Backgrounds Study Bible*, 182.

75 *NIV Cultural Backgrounds Study Bible*, 1621.

76 *NIV Cultural Backgrounds Study Bible*, Page 170.

77 *NIV Cultural Backgrounds Study Bible*, 169.

78 *NIV Cultural Backgrounds Study Bible*, 923.

79 *NIV Archaeological Study Bible*, Page 194.

80 *NIV Cultural Backgrounds Study Bible*, 252.

81 *NIV Archaeological Study Bible*, 194.

82 *NIV Archaeological Study Bible*, 194.

83 *NIV Cultural Backgrounds Study Bible*, 231.

84 *The NIV Study Bible*, (The Zondervan Corporation, 1995): 183.

85 *NIV Cultural Backgrounds Study Bible*, 231–232.

86 "Numbers in Numbers," in *NIV Cultural Backgrounds Study Bible*, 235.

87 Kelli Fleck, *Survey of the Old Testament 1*, The Moody Bible Institute of Chicago (2012): 53.

88 *NIV Cultural Backgrounds Study Bible*, 254.

89 *NIV Cultural Backgrounds Study Bible*, 254.

90 *NIV Cultural Backgrounds Study Bible*, 255.

91 *NIV Cultural Backgrounds Study Bible*, 255.

92 *NIV Cultural Backgrounds Study Bible*, 259–260.

93 *NIV Cultural Backgrounds Study Bible*, 264.

94 *NIV Cultural Backgrounds Study Bible*, 264.

95 *NIV Cultural Backgrounds Study Bible*, 266.

96 *NIV Cultural Backgrounds Study Bible*, 1811.

97 "Balaam," in *NIV Cultural Backgrounds Study Bible*, 268–269.

98 Barry J. Beitzel, *The New Moody Atlas of the Bible*, (2009), 115.

99 Barry J. Beitzel, *The New Moody Atlas of the Bible*, (2009), 122–123.

100 *NIV Archaeological Study Bible*, 252.

101 "The Death of Moses and the Authorship of Deuteronomy," in *NIV Cultural Backgrounds Study Bible*, 356.

102 "Timeline," in *NIV Archaeological Study Bible*, 252.

103 "Timeline," in *NIV Archaeological Study Bible*, 252.

104 "Audience," in *NIV Archaeological Study Bible*, 252.

105 *NIV Cultural Backgrounds Study Bible*, 664.

106 "Timeline," in *NIV Archaeological Study Bible*, 252.

107 "Historical Setting," in *NIV Cultural Backgrounds Study Bible*, 291.

108 "Themes," in *NIV Archaeological Study Bible*, 253.

109 *NIV Cultural Backgrounds Study Bible*, 300.

110 *NIV Cultural Backgrounds Study Bible*, 306–307.

111 *NIV Cultural Backgrounds Study Bible*, 327.

112 *NIV Cultural Backgrounds Study Bible*, 339.

113 *NIV Cultural Backgrounds Study Bible*, 347.

114 *NIV Cultural Backgrounds Study Bible*, 348.

115 *NIV Cultural Backgrounds Study Bible*, 348.

116 *NIV Cultural Backgrounds Study Bible*, 60.

117 *NIV Cultural Backgrounds Study Bible*, 302.

118 *NIV Cultural Backgrounds Study Bible*, 302.

119 *NIV Cultural Backgrounds Study Bible*, 216.

120 *NIV Cultural Backgrounds Study Bible*, 1851.

121 *NIV Cultural Backgrounds Study Bible*, 1842.

122 *NIV Cultural Backgrounds Study Bible*, 198.

123 "Author, Place, and Date of Writing," in *NIV Archaeological Study Bible*, 302.

124 "Timeline," in *NIV Archaeological Study Bible*, 302.

125 "Timeline," in *NIV Archaeological Study Bible*, 302.

126 "Audience," in *NIV Archaeological Study Bible*, 302.

127 "Cultural Facts and Highlights," in *NIV Archaeological Study Bible*, 302.

128 "Historical Background," in *NIV Cultural Backgrounds Study Bible*, 359.

129 "Cultural Facts and Highlights," in *NIV Archaeological Study Bible*, 302.

130 *NIV Cultural Backgrounds Study Bible*, 363.

131 *NIV Cultural Backgrounds Study Bible*, 363.

132 *NIV Cultural Backgrounds Study Bible*, 364.

133 *NIV Cultural Backgrounds Study Bible*, 368.

134 *NIV Cultural Backgrounds Study Bible*, 370.

135 *NIV Cultural Backgrounds Study Bible*, 370.

136 *NIV Cultural Backgrounds Study Bible*, 371.

137 "The Sun Stands Still and the Moon Stops," in *NIV Cultural Backgrounds Study Bible*, 378.

138 *NIV Cultural Backgrounds Study Bible*, 400.

139 *NIV Archaeological Study Bible*, 141–142.

140 *NIV Cultural Backgrounds Study Bible*, 411.

141 *NIV Cultural Backgrounds Study Bible*, 447.

142 *NIV Cultural Backgrounds Study Bible*, 731.

143 "Author, Place and Date of Writing," in *NIV Archaeological Study Bible*, 342.

144 "Author, Place and Date of Writing," in *NIV Archaeological Study Bible*, 342.

145 "The Judges Period," in *NIV Archaeological Study Bible*, 344.

146 "Author, Place and Date of Writing," in *NIV Archaeological Study Bible*, 342.

147 *NIV Cultural Backgrounds Study Bible*, 402.

148 "Cultural Facts and Highlights," in *NIV Archaeological Study Bible*, 342.

149 *Halley's Bible Handbook*, 58.

150 "Timeline," in *NIV Archaeological Study Bible*, 342.

151 *NIV Cultural Backgrounds Study Bible*, 2049.

152 *NIV Cultural Backgrounds Study Bible*, 425.

153 *NIV Cultural Backgrounds Study Bible*, 421.

154 *NIV Cultural Backgrounds Study Bible*, 422.

155 *NIV Cultural Backgrounds Study Bible*, 423–424.

156 *NIV Cultural Backgrounds Study Bible*, 424.

157 *NIV Cultural Backgrounds Study Bible*, 424.

158 *NIV Cultural Backgrounds Study Bible*, 424.

159 *NIV Cultural Backgrounds Study Bible*, 424.

160 *NIV Cultural Backgrounds Study Bible*, 426.

161 *NIV Cultural Backgrounds Study Bible*, 904.

162 "Author, Place, and Date of Writing," in *NIV Archaeological Study Bible*, 386.

163 "Timeline," in *NIV Archaeological Study Bible*, 386.

164 "Timeline," in *NIV Archaeological Study Bible*, 386.

165 "Audience," in *NIV Archaeological Study Bible*, 386.

166 "Cultural Facts and Highlights," in *NIV Archaeological Study Bible*, 386.

167 "Historical Setting," in *NIV Cultural Backgrounds Study Bible*, 448.

168 "Themes," in *NIV Archaeological Study Bible*, 387.

169 *NIV Cultural Backgrounds Study Bible*, 450.

170 *NIV Cultural Backgrounds Study Bible*, 451.

171 *NIV Cultural Backgrounds Study Bible*, 212.

172 *NIV Cultural Backgrounds Study Bible*, 337.

173 *NIV Cultural Backgrounds Study Bible*, 454.

174 *NIV Cultural Backgrounds Study Bible*, 454.

175 *NIV Cultural Backgrounds Study Bible*, 225.

176 "Did You Know?" in *NIV Archaeological Study Bible*, 387.

177 *NIV Cultural Backgrounds Study Bible*, 455.

178 *NIV Cultural Backgrounds Study Bible*, 455.

179 *NIV Cultural Backgrounds Study Bible*, 456.

180 *NIV Cultural Backgrounds Study Bible*, 457–458.

Printed in the United States
By Bookmasters